As the Dust Devils Danced

"God, Pashtun Honor, Opium and Stability
in Uruzgan, Afghanistan"

Jeffrey Crowther

authorHOUSE®

AuthorHouse™
1663 Liberty Drive
Bloomington, IN 47403
www.authorhouse.com
Phone: 1 (800) 839-8640

Published by AuthorHouse 11/30/2015

ISBN: 978-1-5049-6352-7 (sc)
ISBN: 978-1-5049-6353-4 (hc)
ISBN: 978-1-5049-6351-0 (e)

Library of Congress Control Number: 2015919342

Print information available on the last page.

God, grant me the serenity to accept the things I cannot change, the courage to change the things I can, and the wisdom to know the difference.

—Reinhold Niebuhr, American theologian, 1892–1971

Introduction

I held the pod that had oozed the dark opium paste, which had since been scraped and packed away. The special tool with the multiple razor-sharp blades had left the unique diagonal parallel line cut marks. As I turned the pod, I saw four more areas where the same diagonal cut had been made. Stewart, our PRT agricultural advisor, took the pod from me and told me it had been a good harvest of opium this year. While we poured millions of dollars into the region, Uruzgan had become a center of the worldwide illicit opium trade. It is the foundation of their economy. Everything and everyone is tied to it.

I looked west over the mountain toward the town of Deh Rawud, where Mullah Omar, the spiritual leader of the Taliban, grew up under the harsh hand of his uncle, who was also his stepfather. He would leave there for Kandahar and later bring the Taliban movement back to Uruzgan and all of Afghanistan. Though the Taliban would at first outlaw the opium trade, they would later embrace it, as no other export of Afghanistan brings in so much money to this extremely underdeveloped country. Whoever is in power, locally and nationally, must control it, or others will exploit the wealth it brings and take their place.

In the heat of the day, several dust devils spiraling hundreds of feet into the air were dancing across the sprawling, dusty landscape between my perch on Camp Ripley and the green, irrigated farmlands just outside the Uruzgan provincial capital of Tarin Kowt. The "nesh," the poppy harvest, was over, and the fighting season in Afghanistan had begun its deadly annual cycle. The opium these poppy plants produced was opposed by the international forces because it was a money source for the now-insurgent Taliban forces. However, with over ten thousand hectares under cultivation in Uruzgan, I knew everyone of consequence in the region had a hand in the trade, especially the local warlord and soon-to-be provincial chief of police, Matiullah Khan.

As the rule of law advisor for the Uruzgan Provincial Reconstruction Team, I was faced with the challenge of creating a sustainable justice system, where it was unavoidable that Matiullah, who was hated by many tribes in the region, needed to be central to that system. In the chaos of conflict, there can be no justice without security. I kept Niebuhur's prayer attached to my e-mail correspondence as a daily reminder of the limits I would encounter. This is a piece of the story of a region of the world where massive armies have waxed and waned across its landscape as the people, just like the dust devils, have performed their timeless, swirling dance, positioning themselves to use the invaders' power to their advantage until the inevitable withdrawal occurred.

Uruzgan, Afghanistan:
A Land of Loyalty, Opium, and God

"Tarburwali (Pashtu for the rivalry of agnatic cousins) … the position of leadership itself is structurally weak. It lacked the right of command and so depended on the ability to persuade others to follow. (No Afghan feels anyone else is above him.) It is tough being a chief of a people whom you had to cajole into action and where criticism is constant. For this reason religious leaders were often more successful than tribal ones in uniting large groups. Coming from outside the system and calling on God's authority, they could circumvent tribal rivalries.
—Thomas Barfield, *Afghanistan, A Cultural and Political History*

Barfield paints a picture of how politics work in Afghanistan. Similar to the international policy of large nations, there are constant negotiations, with the threat of force always lingering in the background. At the time of the 2001 US invasion following the horrific attack on the World Trade Center, Afghanistan was in ruins. Decades of internal conflict, exasperated by the Soviet invasion to prop up the failing Communist regime in Kabul, precipitated the civil war between tribal leaders, which ended in the supremacy of the Taliban movement. Our well-intentioned efforts to reconstruct—or should I say, construct—the civil society that Western nations wanted to see in Afghanistan, were based upon teams of civilian and military personnel in each province of the country. By 2010, our efforts had proved unable to create a fully functioning central government. However, we had created a parallel government made up of Provincial Reconstruction Teams (PRTs). Now it was time to dismantle them without the country imploding into another round of civil war. I walked into that effort as a senior rule of law advisor with the US Department of State, assigned to the remote region of Uruzgan Province.

My assignment was to assist the people of Uruzgan with the development of a justice system consistent with the new Afghan Constitution. Uruzgan is a region of Afghanistan where the Kabul government always faced a population that harbored resistance to its influence but needed its cooperation. A mountainous region whose people possess a fierce independent pride, a place rebels have run to and fought from for centuries. Populated by multiple tribes and subtribes their loyalties ebb and flow based on patronage and the Pashtunwali honor code, all wrapped in a sense of proper Islam. It is essential to understand that Islam is in a state of flux in Uruzgan as the conflict between the centuries-old Hanifi sharia and the relatively new Wahhabi sharia, grounded in the old Salafism, turned into a sharia legal theory by Ahmad Ibn Taymiyya (1262–1328) and promoted by the Talib, rages in the land. It is a high-altitude desert where crops are grown by hand-dug irrigation canals near the glacier streams making their way down from the mountain ranges toward the Helmand River. It is an exhausting effort, and the crop that gives the greatest return for such efforts is the opium poppy.

As I read Barfield while preparing to go to Afghanistan, I couldn't help thinking his words concerning what we saw as a backward country seemed to be torn right out of the headlines of news about our own government. Does not our president come under constant criticism? Is not our government formed on the basis of persons of different priorities and ideologies coming together in state houses and Congress, arguing over what should be the law of the land? Do not our politicians reach out to God's Word as the basis for their stand on an issue of the day? Is this "Tarburwali" not the basis for people governing themselves? When you place this thought alongside the tribal organizations of South Afghanistan, do we not have the foundation of democracy much as existed back in the ancient Greek city-states?

However, on the ground in Uruzgan was a basic government of one city-state, which was not receiving much support from the national government of Afghanistan. Uruzgan resembled disenfranchised communities of other nations and in other times. Like populations in Colombia and Mexico over the last half century, as well as many regions of the U.S.A., especially urban immigrant ghettos of the late

2

1800s and early 1900s, Uruzgan was ripe for those willing to be better providers than the government in Kabul. Though to be clear, just like the gangsters of alcohol prohibition in the United States, unless those in political power in Kabul got their cut of the action, the local powerbrokers wouldn't last long.

What astounded me was that those being sent into Afghanistan, putatively to develop a civil society, seemingly failed to read much of anything concerning Barfield's research. Instead, they read books on the Taliban, a modern phenomenon born of Wahhabi Islam imported into Afghanistan through the students, the Talib. Many Talib had been orphaned and sent to the Saudi-supported schools, called madrassas, in Pakistan during the civil war that brought the Soviets to Afghanistan to prevent the then-communist Kabul government from falling. These students were broken from their families and tribes; they then came back to Afghanistan and formed their own tribe, in a sense, based on the kinship they shared in those madrassas. This was natural, for in the rural regions of Afghanistan, kinship relationships are crucial to survival.

This fraternity of Wahhabi brothers was sympathetic to a similar Islamic movement that would find fertile ground under their protection, known as Al-Qaida, Arabic for "the base." Their Sharia, Wahhabism, was the base of proper Islamic behavior that they believed all Muslims should follow. The leader of these Talib grew up in the Afghan province of Uruzgan in a small town west of the provincial capital called Deh Rawud. He is known to the world as Mullah Omar.

Through my conversations concerning Mullah Omar with the longtime district governor of Deh Rawud, Kalifa Sadat, there emerged a picture of a young boy who endured a harsh childhood. At a young age, Omar came under his uncle's roof when, according to Pashtunwali and Islamic tradition, his uncle married his brother's wife—Omar's mother—when she was widowed. His uncle was a mullah at a local mosque, where a rigid Islamic sharia—possibly the traditional Hanbal sharia, mixed with the ancient Pashtunwali—was taught. Kalifa's stories of abuse, both physical and mental, at the hands of his uncle left me no doubt that Mullah Omar fit the classic picture of an adult shaped by childhood violence.

Afghanistan is a land where in 2011, 60 percent of the population was under the age of twenty-five, 50 percent was under the age of eighteen, and 44.5 percent was under the age of fourteen. Years of violent conflict claimed the older men, while others just emigrated to avoid the violence. The Provincial Reconstruction Team (PRT) structure in Afghanistan, unlike Iraq, had actually created a parallel government alongside that of the duly constituted Afghan government—which we call the Government of the Islamic Republic of Afghanistan, or GIRoA. This parallel government formed because GIRoA had not been able to stand above the tribes and administer transparent and just governance with rule of law as its base. However, given the history of the area and Barfield's research findings, had any Kabul-based government ever accomplished that? Had not all of them reached accommodation with and not power over the rural regions? Hadn't this region always operated much like a large grouping of organized crime families, where the money was always disbursed through deals and backroom negotiations, with the threat of violence always in the air if negotiations should fail?

Did we have an unrealistic vision of what civil society could be in Afghanistan at this time? The money provided by coalition partners to operate the government wasn't flowing down to the governmental agencies at the provincial and district levels. This was due to the high level of what we call corrupt behavior—but what their culture sees as normal taking of money and using it for their networks that secure their positions. In our efforts to keep the provincial governments viable, the PRT had been making up the shortfalls. A vicious cycle had been started and now it had to come to an end. Our instructions were to break that connection and mentor accordingly.

When I arrived, I sensed the frustration of those who held similar roles as I did. Most of them didn't understand the strength of culture's hold on societal development. This led to a frustrated effort focused on "programs in a box" that targeted only some very fluid top issues but failed to address the depth of the culture beneath, and so attempted solutions that the underlying culture wouldn't accept. They failed to see that the Taliban movement, though an indigenous political movement, was itself struggling to gain long-term acceptance within the Afghan cultures. I emphasize *cultures* because Afghanistan was home to a wide breadth of active tribes, whereas the Taliban movement was mostly of Pashtu origin.

During my two and a half years in Afghanistan, I saw our own efforts being influenced both by the tribes who had our ears and those who didn't—to the point that by 2012, I heard that it was clear that we were dealing with two Afghanistan nations. One was the Tajik and Uzbek in the north, where Kabul lay, and the other the Pashtu that dominated the south, which was Kandahar City-centric. Kabul-centric thinking can be dangerous. Afghanistan historically has been a confederacy of tribes that reached a consensus through various means, one being the *loya jirga*, concerning how the nation should move forward. The loya jirga approved the United States and its partners maintaining a military presence in the country, but President Karzai again played the Afghan renegotiating game that could have led to the entire international community pulling out.

In February 2014, Karzai released several hundred Talban fighters from Bagram Prison over the objections of the United States. This was obviously a move reflecting ongoing negotiations among the tribal groups, as Afghanistan began shedding the presence of its latest invader and returning to its norm—though not ours. The constant deal making that epitomizes Afghan culture is not understood by the outside world. On April 5, 2014, over 60 percent of the Afghan population defied the threats of the Taliban by standing for hours at the polling stations. President Harmid Karzai became the first Afghan leader to leave office alive. No clear winners emerged, so runoff elections were held between Ashraf Ghani Ahmadzai and Abdullah Abdullah.

Ashraf Ghani comes from the same tribe as the president installed by the Soviets during their occupation of Afghanistan, Mohammad Najibullah Ahmadzai. That particular tribe has strong ties to the Western Tribal Area in Pakistan and is part of the Ghilzai Pashtu tribe in Afghanistan, which is the largest in Uruzgan with strong ties to the Taliban. The Pashtu have for a long time been seen as the natural heir to the national leadership. Abdullah Abdullah comes from the Northern Tajik tribes and was closely allied with Ahmad Shah Massoud, "The Lion of the North," the leader of the Northern Alliance who was killed by Al-Qaida just prior to the September 11, 2001 attack on the World Trade Center. Since the Taliban is mainly a Pashtu movement, one can see the immediate conflict between the two candidates and their supporters.

Dr. Abdullah Abdullah lost in the runoff and immediately claimed fraud, which resulted in a UN-monitored recount. Claims of fraud were thrown around the entire time the recount was underway, and even when the elections results were confirmed, Dr. Abdullah Abdullah refused to concede. Thus began a period of tense negotiations lasting over six months and resulting in a typical Afghan power-sharing deal where tribal leaders reach consensus with one another to move forward in a manner where both groups reap benefits. The election's results were finally honored, putting Ashraf Ghani in office as president. However, moments after Ashraf Ghani Ahmadzai took the oath of office, he swore in Abdullah Abdullah as "chief executive," creating the sharing of power that defused the election tensions that had threatened to spark violence between the country's north and southeast. Never mind that the Afghan Constitution has no such position as chief executive. The longstanding Pashtu national leadership role had been maintained within a new confederacy framework thousands of years old.

This ancient confederacy of tribes into one "nation" is very complicated to the Western mind because all the major tribes have several subtribes under their umbrellas. As you drill down into these tribal structures, emergence of family ties and kinship becomes very important. Marriages are family/political alliances, and given the acceptance of polygamy for the men of the tribes, knowing all their wives is strategically important to know all their alliances. This is extremely difficult given the social taboo of discussing the female members of the family with outsiders. It is so offensive to the Afghan males to be asked about their female family members that it can cause a violent reaction that can get one killed. Women are a symbol of family honor and they are protected in the extreme, leading to what we in the West would call a lack of freedom and abuse of basic human rights.

The loyalty to family and tribe is exemplified by the phrase, "I against my brother; my brother and I against our cousin; my brother, cousin, and I against the tribe; our tribe against all other tribes, and all tribes against outsiders." This creates a society where nothing gets done without all the family ties being considered, so negotiations are constant and ongoing and subject to renegotiation. Communication is not direct and "in your face" but laced with suggestions and done in a storytelling manner. Knowing the foundations of the stories told is important, thus an outsider is immediately at a disadvantage, and miscommunications are a problem. We continually refused to accept this cultural reality of things being in a constant state of negotiations as we were attempting to build civil society in Afghanistan. Time, and I mean a long time, is what it takes to influence the people of Afghanistan. Outsiders don't have the patience to stay that long. Much as Ho Chi Min stated to the US forces in Vietnam, and Gandhi did to the British during India's subcontinent struggle to obtain self-rule, "Someday all outsiders will go home on their own accord. We will just wait you out and in the process make it painful for you to stay, generation after generation." In the meantime, the Afghans who work with outsiders will do so to their tribal/family network's benefit, all the time maintaining all necessary relationships for future changes. All Afghan leaders in Uruzgan that I worked with had family members associated with the Taliban at some level. It may have been a third cousin twice removed, but they knew who they were and communicated with them when needed. This cooperation was exemplified as winter approached in 2011. The Taliban reached out to the Uruzgan strongman and newly named provincial chief of police, Matiullah Khan, for safe passage back to Pakistan before the winter snows blocked the mountain passages. Matiullah let it be known that they had three days of safe passage. After that, he would kill them. The implications that he knew where they were, who they where, and the fact that he was allowing safe passage for three days sent a clear message— Matiullah was the one who held their destiny in Uruzgan. These favors and threats were the poker chips for future negotiations, depending on how the winds of change blow. Mullah Omar, the Taliban leader, is faced with this same dynamic and it will play heavily into his ability to bring the Taliban back into a power position as ISAF leaves the region.

The overarching struggle in Afghanistan is that of Islam, and what sharia means to the population. Offend an Afghan's understanding of Islam and Allah at the risk of your life being taken immediately. In Uruzgan, reference to the prophet of Islam, Mohammad, was always done by the phrase "peace be upon him" and not his name. This is a sign of extreme conservative Islam, for even the mention of his name can be seen as worshipping him instead of Allah and therefore forbidden as a form of idolatry. However, that very issue is where I believe the struggle lies in Afghanistan, and therefore the outsiders coming with their "constitution" as the law, the modern sharia, were making the same mistake the former Afghan communist government made when it pushed communist-based rule of law into the rural regions, sparking the religious war in retaliation for such action.

Islam came late to Afghanistan in the sense that it began in the seventh century but wasn't complete until the late, very late, nineteenth century. It also came into the region of already well-established cultural legal systems based on tribal affiliations. The one I worked with in Uruzgan was "Pashtunwali" or the Pashtun honor code by which they defined who they are. That is, what does it mean to be or do things in a Pashtu manner that brings honor and therefore justice to the family and tribe? Other tribes in Afghanistan and Pakistan have similar ways within their tribal groups. Much as Christianity absorbed pagan and tribal customs into the faith in order that the faith be accepted, so did Islam in Afghanistan. However, here is the critical point where the conflict between Pashtunwali and Islam lies. Both are connected to legal structures that are so connected to the faith and the honor code that the culture of being Pashtu has areas where it is in conflict with the proper path of a Muslim, the sharia. However, the preferred law struggle doesn't end there. There is a region-wide conflict between the progressive Sunni schools of sharia developed over centuries versus the relatively newer Salafist sharia. Salafism (the way of the elders) was introduced as a sharia in the 1200s by Ibn Taymiyya. Taymiyya look to Mohammad's time and three generations thereafter as the guiding principle as to how a Muslim should live their lives. In particular, he bristled under the rule of the invading Mongol rulers of today's modern day Iraq, who had converted to Shia Islam. Under the three main schools of Sunni sharia a Muslim was duty bound to support the government. Taymiyya didn't wish to do this and his Salafist approach allowed for the individual Muslim to rebel against the rulers. Salafism was adopted in the mid to late 1700s by the Saud tribe of the Arabian peninsula as they embraced Taymiyya's disciple Muhammad al-Wahhab. This struggle is at the center of the conflict in the Middle East as well as Afghanistan. Wahhabi sharia, the Wahhabi Islamic path for one's life, was the foundation of the madrassas, founded by the Saudis in Pakistan, where the young Afghan orphan boys were sent to during the long Afghan Civil War. This Wahhabi/Salafist sharia is the foundation of the Al-Qaida (the base of Islam), Taliban (the students), and the Islamic State of Iraq and Syria movement, which today, in 2015, is finding its way into Helmand Province of Afghanistan. These forces converging in Afghanistan caused great complexities of defining the base upon which "Afghan law" can find cultural legitimacy in the eyes of the people of the region. This deeply rooted cultural struggle was totally at odds and undermined efforts to bring a "constitutional sharia" represented by the Afghan Constitution, no matter how well intentioned, into that mix.

When the Afghan Constitution was drafted, it was done so in conformity with Hanifi sharia, the main school of Sunni sharia in Afghanistan, which by Western standards is moderate and progressive. The problem is that the greater portion of the population doesn't even know what proper Hanifi sharia is. They still live in a society that blended all things Afghan with Islam, creating a hybrid Islamic sharia that absorbed the Pashtunwali-type legal systems that exist at the tribal levels. Therefore, proper Islamic behavior includes honor killings, keeping women covered in burkas, and *baad*, the practice of giving daughters as compensation to settle wrongs committed by members of a family against other families. To not do such things is viewed as anti-Islamic and dealt with harshly. My Iraqi friends would say the people of Afghanistan only read half of the Koran to express this oppression of women.

There was a lack of understanding of where the "rule of law" struggle was taking place. in the multiple layers of "law" in Uruzgan, Afghanistan. The embassy level of coalition partners was focused on delivering legal education directed at introducing the law of Afghanistan under the new Afghan Constitution. Though based on Hanifi sharia there was strong opposition to the constitution for being un-Islamic. We at UPRT felt that the focus needed to be on their traditional justice deliver methods first then mentoring toward the constitution as supporting the traditional. Our obvious goal was to have the government legal systems accepted and used by the community. We had the support of the Uruzgan Province chief judge on this approach for it fit his efforts to combat Wahhabi sharia promoted by the Taliban. The resistance at the embassy to this approach was so great that I could be assured of a heated discussion by any suggestion that I was focusing on my chief judge's commitment to having the tribal elders educated in the difference between Pashtunwali and Hanifi sharia as a first step to bringing them to accept that the constitution was merely the Hanifi sharia written down. He used to say to me that the Taliban promoted the wrong sharia. The fact that he understood that the struggle was which sharia his people would follow made him a very dangerous man to the Taliban. That fear of Hanifi sharia winning over the Wahhabi sharia made him a target of three assassination attempts, one that took the life of one of his sons and wounded him and his other son. Allah was the trump card to all other discussions, and he knew it. I was to learn much from him.

This was the quagmire I was entering. I was determined to create a cultural approach. I would find great resistance from the Western minds. They looked at this ancient civilization as backward and undemocratic, as if diseased and in need of a cure. I settled on Niebuhr's serenity prayer as a guide, "God, grant me the serenity to accept the things I cannot change, the courage to change the things I can, and the wisdom to know the difference," and a "Let go and let God" approach, opening my mind to what riches I could find to teach me what I needed to be able to become a part of their solution for a stable society that could open the doors of peaceful coexistence once again. Little did I know at that time that I would look to the drug cartels of Colombia and Mexico run by Pablo Escobar and Joaquin "El Chapo" Guzman as a first step toward creating that peaceful coexistence between the tribes of Uruzgan and the emerging criminal justice system with its mixture of holy men, judges, and a drug warlord turned chief of the provincial police.

The Kabul Cough and Other Surprises

Late on an early December evening, after several weeks of training, I found myself at Washington Dulles International Airport waiting on a flight to the Middle East. A similar cast of characters, reminiscent of my travels to Baghdad via Kuwait City, had gathered at the gate. They were comprised of mostly Westerners working in Dubai and US contractor employees going to Afghanistan. The few that were obvious locals to the region held the first-class tickets. The flight to Dubai was about fifteen hours, which for those of us sitting in tourist class became much like a Chinese drip torture experience. The US-flagged carriers worked on a for-profit model requiring such accommodations. I would have the luxury of flying Emirates, the Saudi Arabian airline, one time in the two-plus years of traveling to Dubai. Tourist class in a government-subsidized Emirates aircraft was equal to business in a US carrier.

After unfolding my stiff body out of the aircraft in Dubai, I entered the Las Vegas of the Middle East. Such opulence and design in an airport I had never seen. Whatever you want you can get there. Having a very early flight in the morning, I chose a pleasant hotel with a good breakfast buffet. Unlike the Iraq experience going through Kuwait, we were on our own. Dubai is a very safe city and well-traveled by Europeans. There would be no handlers and no, thank God, brutal C-130 flight into Kabul. We were to fly into Kabul on an Afghan commercial airline called Safi Air. There were other airlines we could have taken, like Fly Dubai, but the US embassy had a contract with Safi, probably as part of our efforts to support Afghan business, which may or may not have been the "best" price.

The flight into Kabul was non-eventful but crowded. Entering the Kabul International Airport (KIA) facility, it was clear Afghanistan is a poor country. However, as my time there extended the stories of the multimillions of US dollars skimmed from projects around the country that illegally passed through KIA—and no the ironic acronym didn't go unnoticed[1]—went from the amazing to the absurd. An estimated $600 million a month in assorted currency left Afghanistan in pouches and bags through KIA. I came to view such information as an example of how tribal politics weakens a nation and is destructive to a democracy. I can't say it was all skimmed money, because of the large opium drug trade that goes on there. All one had to do was declare the amount of cash you were taking out of the country. Also, there were several VIP areas where questions were not asked. When the United States insisted on placing bill counters and scanners connected to a database to compare the bills used in US project payments to those leaving the country, enabling capturing those misappropriated dollars, the Afghans trained to use them often did not do so or found them "broken." Millions of taxpayer dollars flowed freely into the bosses' foreign bank accounts. It was a standing joke within the Afghan population about the Karzai families' multimillion dollar homes in Dubai. Lack of concern in the American citizenry of what was really going on in Afghanistan created a troubling silence to these well-known stories in Afghanistan.

After clearing customs, I found the US embassy driver waiting on all of us destined for the embassy. We walked across the driveways that came to the front doors of KIA, now sealed to avoid a vehicle-borne improvised explosive device (VBIED), to our awaiting armored SUV for our drive to the embassy. Traveling through the very crowded streets of Kabul, I was very aware of the ease at which any pedestrian or passenger

---

[1.] KIA is the acronym for "killed in action."

on a motorcycle could come by and stick an explosive device to the vehicle. This was confirmed by the several checkpoints, culminated by a bomb dog and chemical swipe detection process to enter the US embassy's controlled area, we had to go through to get into the Western nations' embassy area of Kabul. Time and time again we would be given briefings concerning what to do if large crowds gathered around our vehicle, preventing our vehicle from moving. We were also briefed about having the US embassy Diplomatic Security command post phone number in our cell phones and our GPS 911 at the ready during travel through Kabul between the many facilities we would use during our time in Afghanistan.

Arriving at the temporary housing at the US embassy, I ran into several persons I had gone through training with. I was the only one slated for Uruzgan. As I was going through the check-in process, receiving my cell phone and other electronic devices, the Afghans working the desks would ask me which province I was being sent to. When I responded Uruzgan, they all, and I mean all, just looked at me and said something to the effect of, "Oh that is a very dangerous place." I thought, *Well I'm in for it now.*

Walking from location to location on the extended embassy complex took your breath, literally. The mountain scenery was something to behold, and the elevation of almost 5,900 feet (1,800 meters), slightly higher than Tarin Kowt's approximate 4,300 feet (1,300 of meters), required adjusting to the thin air. On clear days, the view was magnificent with the converging Asmai and Sherdawaza mountain ranges surrounding Kabul sporting snowcapped peaks. This 3,500-year-old city sits in a triangle-shaped valley where five different mountain passes created a natural ancient crossroads for the silk road trade. This led to a city that flourished during the days of land travel, as it was a natural center for trade and of course the payment of tariffs to allow that trade to continue on. However, as air transport grew, Kabul became less important as a route for trade. Afghanistan's southern city of Kandahar, the local name for Alexander who had conquered Afghanistan in 331 BC, rose in importance as a refueling point for rotary winged aircraft. However, as long-range flight rose in the aviation world, Kandahar's importance fell, leaving Afghanistan once again a very isolated region.

December is quite cold in Kabul, and clear days can be rare because of the poverty of the region and because the burning of something, anything flammable, is the main source of home heating. Wood comes into the city from surrounding regions since Kabul's wooded area had long since been stripped bare. One of the many projects that were instituted was the reforesting of the sloops around Kabul to prevent soil erosion and therefore mudslides. Animal and human fecal material has long been used as fuel in austere societies. Buffalo chips on the American prairie were such a fuel source. In the Himalaya regions of Ladak, India, and Nepal, the Buddhist monks constructed elevated latrines to capture the human dropping for both fertilizer and fuel. But those were small population situations, and fecal matter in the air didn't cause any serious health issues due to the abundant airflow. However, in a high altitude valley with a population of approximately 3.2 million people, it creates a significant health issue. Those who actually worked at the embassy labeled a rather chronic cough many of them endured as the "Kabul cough." I contracted it during the one week I spent there. It was time to go. However, unlike Iraq, the transport at such altitudes, over longer distances, wasn't going to be helicopters.

Embassy Air, a charter service tendered by a contractor named Air Charter Services, was basically our own private fixed-wing aircraft service. Originally the embassy had a person who we were assigned to as a "field support officer." They handled all the ground transport and dealt with all the issues at the embassy, such as housing, when we came in from the field. We would book our flights online, and the field support officer would handle all the rest. The process worked great, and travel for my first year and a half went very smoothly. That would change later as some good-idea fairy, looking for something to do, created a nightmare of a website that was supposed to create a coordinated, one-stop procedure online to simplify the process and create better accountability for where the field personnel were. Many experienced being stranded at the Embassy Air terminal late at night without transport to the embassy, or a vehicle would be present, but your name wasn't on the list. I had several conversations with the motor pool supervisor who couldn't understand how we arrived at Kabul without his knowledge. There were times where he backed down from refusing to send a vehicle to get me only when I said, "I'm done talking and will call in my concerns to the Diplomatic Security Command Center." There was no way they were going to allow us to be placed in a possible kidnapping situation late at night trying to get to the embassy by some other means. Needless to say, I avoided going to Kabul as much as possible.

However, on this occasion, as if on cue, I was able to reconnect with many from my PRT from Camp Taji, Iraq. Colleagues who, like me, were in transit or on temporary assignments or had permanent assignments at the US embassy in Kabul. Christopher from USAID would soon be down in Helmand Province with the Brits and US Marines heading up that program there. Mary-Denise had just finished up a temporary assignment. That girl had more hostile fire time than most soldiers between Iraq and AFG. She related stories in her mix of Georgetown intelligentsia and street language that had us all in stiches. A nod to the well-known but underreported abuse of young males by Afghan men, she related a story of how on a walk to a meeting, the youngest male member of the army unit escorting her had to worry more about getting grabbed by the local men than she did. She followed that one up with another about a rocket attack that occurred while she was showering that drove her into the bunker with soaking wet hair and barely clothed as she grabbed what she could on the way there. Malcolm was working USAID in Kabul, and we all were just glad to be back in each other's company. We spent some time at the Duck and Cover, an embassy employee watering hole, and then retired to Malcolm's CHU (container housing unit) to spend time with each other. Battle buddies are precious cargo in life, and you tend not to want to share them with others. There was also a real feeling that Afghanistan was much more dangerous than our time in Iraq ever was. We certainly wanted to hold onto each other for just a moment before we parted ways once again.

Multinational Base Tarin Kowt, Uruzgan: Godt Morgen; G'Day, Mate; and Howdy

The laughter of the night with the gang was still in my head the next morning. Flying out of Kabul on a cold December 12 morning in a small aircraft with seating for no more than fifteen, but carrying only three, was quite a treat. Climbing over the mountaintops surrounding Kabul, I was able to see why this location was once such a crossroad of trade. Unlike a large aircraft, this aircraft was very susceptible to the air turbulence, and we were flying in the clouds more often than above them. If you had any fear of flying, this would challenge your ability to hold it together. The farther south we flew, the clearer the sky became. The awesome rough beauty of the terrain was a sight to behold. The flight was about three hours, and the low altitude of the aircraft gave me a good view of the makeup of the land and villages below. All was brown and barren except in small valleys where the glacial runoffs created the water flowing down to the Helmand River. There I could see small patches of green lining the banks of the flows and irrigation canals creating square areas waiting on the spring planting. You could see villages on either side of a steep mountain ridge. I was to learn later that though they may be only a few miles apart, these ridges kept the inhabitants from meeting directly. They would travel downriver until the flows converged. There another village or town was erected, which became the hub of activity where inhabitants of the two villages converged in commerce. The steep mountains had paths running along the ridgelines and then down the steep edges at different points. Probably from goat and foot traffic, for nothing else would be out in that remote region traversing those ridges.

As the aircraft started to descend, the Tarin Kowt (TK) bowl came into view. Tarin Kowt is a city of about ten thousand people. It sits surrounded by steep mountain ridges to the west, arcing over to the southeast, with openings through mountain passes to the south. This topography would cause winter cloud formations to settle in the bowl. The airfield at Multinational Base Tarin Kowt (MNBTK) didn't have the instrumentation to safely bring in aircraft through what I would later describe as a giant marshmallow, clouds that sat on top of the base and surrounding ridges. Landing was always at the pilot's discretion, and slamming either onto the deck as the cloud sat twenty feet off the runway or into the steep mountain walls surrounding the area didn't appeal to any of the pilots. However, on this bright December day of 2010, all was clear, and it was clean landing onto a runway that was mostly hard soil except for the last hundred yards or so. A completed concrete runway was about a year away.

MNBTK runway under the marshmallow cloud

We taxied off the end of the runway onto a stone-covered docking area where I was greeted by Ted, the senior US State Department member on Uruzgan PRT, and George from USAID. Behind him was a large contingent of Afghan officials and an honor guard. I must have had a puzzled look on my face, for Ted immediately told me the new provincial governor (PGOV) was arriving on a plane that just landed behind us. Ted spoke Dari, so he wanted to stick around to greet him and introduce himself. The new PGOV was Omar Sharizad, and his recent appointment had come after Uruzgan's former PGOV, Jan Mohamad Khan (a.k.a. JMK), had been removed almost a year earlier at the insistence of the Dutch who held the ISAF Command at MNBTK at that time. Jan Mohamad Khan was a local leader who had saved President Hamid Karzai's life during an assassination attempt years before. When Karzai took office, he repaid the debt by giving Jan Mohamad the PGOV position in Uruzgan. When I say repaid, I mean just that. At a briefing at a rule of law conference that I would attend in October 2011, the resident FBI agent at the embassy informed us that "all PGOV positions are purchased" and that a border province governorship goes for about $5 million. "Don't feel sorry for those who make the investment, for they are able to recover that amount in three months." Uruzgan had ten thousand hectares of poppy under cultivation. One kilogram of opiate paste brought $800 at the local market by the time I left in 2013. Omar may have been looking to cash in on what Jan Mohamad had coveted, but any return on the investment would depend on his ability to balance the players in the region.

Karzai and Jan Mohammad came from the Popolzai, a subtribe under the Durrani tribe. Jan Mohammad ruled the area brutally. In the process of disarming the area, he drove the Ghilzai tribal groups, the largest in the area, into the arms of the Taliban. This man still exerted huge influence over the area through his nephew, who had cleverly aligned himself, to his advantage, with the US Special Forces. His name was Matiullah Khan. Matiullah controlled the poppy in the TK area and was determined to control all of Uruzgan. Additionally, JMK's Deputy PGOV had been running things in his absence while awaiting the new PGOV. This had kept things in limbo for some time. The fact that JMK's deputy stayed on as deputy governor after Sharizad arrived didn't help the situation. Uruzganis are suspicious of all outsiders, and the PGOV would not be an exception. I would see this play out through the chief judge of Uruzgan many times over the next two-plus years. Omar Sharizad's PGOV tenure was doomed from the start, and I would be there long enough to follow it to the predictable end. On this day, however, it was all one big hospitable welcome for the incoming PGOV.

Ted made his introduction to the new PGOV with the usual struggle between the Pashto language the governor spoke and the Dari Ted was speaking. This dual use of national languages afflicts all Afghans with a sense of division. He introduced me around to some of the people he knew who had come to welcome the PGOV, and then we were off to my new home for the next two and a half years in our one and only vehicle, a Toyota SUV. While bouncing along the rough road, George and I got to know each other a bit, and it was the start of one of the better relationships I would develop while there. Rounding the corner of the runway and starting up the hill into Camp Holland, I could see more of MNBTK. MNBTK was a conglomerate of HESCO barriers, CONEX containers, T walls, and what the Dutch had labeled "chalets." HESCO barriers are an ingenious British device—a folded combination of heavy wire fencing and cloth that comes in many sizes. When unfolded and stuffed with dirt and rocks, they make a solid barrier anywhere from three to about six or eight feet square and three to ten feet tall. All you need is to start your first row and then open the rather light HESCO, place it on top of the row that is already filled, and then start filling it up to create the next row above it. The process doesn't take long, and there is no need for pouring concrete. The cloth will eventually disintegrate, or we would tear them apart, spilling the dirt right back onto the ground, thus fulfilling our commitment to return the base to the way it was prior to our arrival.

The chalets were constructed as heavily fortified bomb shelters. They were mobile containers made of steel several inches thick, outfitted with lights, electrical hookups, and air-conditioner/heating units with doors so heavy that it felt like you were being closed into a meat locker when they slammed closed. They were set side by side and across from each other with the doors facing each other. Then huge steel plates creating an overhead connection between the two facing containers formed a roof over the space between the containers, thus creating a long hall. Above that was a pitched corrugated steel roof placed on top of the entire container setup. The resulting multiple housing units were then surrounded by HESCO barriers filled with earth. The openings created at either end of the hallway were closed off with plywood, and a doorway established at each end with an additional HESCO wall outside blocked any direct entrance into the hallway. There was just enough room to walk between the HESCO wall and the HESCO barriers set up against the exterior of the outermost containers, to squeeze a person and his or her gear into this rocket-proof structure. Unlike the thin-skinned structures found on most US bases, these structures were the rocket shelters. Very nice in the middle of the night when you were in bed and the incoming alarm went off. You could just roll over and go back to sleep, if you even heard the alarm through the thick walls.

I was taken to chalet 17, room 17, which had a combination lock with the convenient code of 1717. The room held a USAID representative, Jason Katz, who had the distinction of holding the record for the most time in Uruzgan. I would set up in the room next to him for the two weeks he had remaining on post. When he did leave, shortly before Christmas, he would say two years was too long to be in Uruzgan. I would break that by several months, but Stu from the United States Department of Agriculture (USDA) would record the longest time there. Stu had the good fortune of being there during the last days with the Dutch. He had gone out to the surrounding areas with them and inspected the different crops, opium included, under cultivation. Often that meant sleeping out under the stars in some rather remote areas. Stu and I would share some great times together. His greatest contribution to our life on MNBTK was creating the "Taj Mah Deck," the envy of MNBTK located on Camp

Ripley. The structure combined the five US State Department CHUs (container housing units), and later two more from a USAID NGO, in such a way that we had a two-story structure with four personnel CHUs, two multiple-bunk CHUs for the frequent state and SF transit folks, our own television lounge, and a great view of the sunsets over the western mountains from the attached deck. It was a sight to behold, always drawing the finest among the Special Ops troops. We worked a deal with the US Special Forces commander at the time to place the two Green Beret officers we worked with the most in the lower CHUs, in exchange for getting hooked up to the Camp Ripley power grid and Armed Forces Network (AFN) that broadcast stateside television programing. There is nothing like getting up at five o'clock on Monday morning to catch the Sunday afternoon NFL games. This arrangement worked out well because the deck turned into a great evening meeting place to work out the tribal governance and rule of law issues in the remote areas the SF Village Stability Operations were working. The young men working those remote areas in small groups were constantly on my mind as they worked with the village elders. A tent village surrounded the deck, where Navy SEALS roamed and the SF activities were supported. The Osprey tilt-winged aircraft coming and going in the middle of the night shook the CHUs, and you got used to the norm of their nighttime activities.

Tent City and selfie of the author

The main challenge was making your way down the steps in the dark of night to get to the Dixie or "Loo", which was Aussie for portapotty, without breaking your leg.

Stu and the Taj Mah Deck

Taj Mah Deck

On Camp Holland, the chalets were laid out in straight rows with a two-container unit latrine each, containing two showers, two toilets, and one urinal between every other chalet. At this time, the latrines were co-ed. The Dutch were still acting as the mayor of the camp, and their culture doesn't blink an eye over men and women sharing such facilities at the same time. That would change with time as the Australians took over running the mayor's post. However, it was interesting to observe the voluntary, almost natural, courtesy given to not imposing upon the other sex. These were not the bomb-proof containers the chalets were made from and tragically easily penetrated by shrapnel from an explosion. Several Dutch female soldiers were severally injured, some fatally, when a rocket hit just outside of the latrine unit they were using.

Covering the ground between these chalets were small stones, a little smaller than one's fist. There were worn pathways. Nonetheless, hardy boots were a necessity to prevent twisting your ankle, especially at night. Throughout the camp, this chalet concept was employed to create all the office working areas. It was a little over a quarter-mile walk from chalet 17 to the PRT's two working chalets. In between the housing village and the work area was a town square, so to speak. Two well-used volleyball courts, a dining facility (DFAC), and an EU military USO-style facility named the Windmill. Both of those were put together using the bomb-proofed containers. They reminded me of Legos. You could remove the side or ends and arrange them to create large, open rooms, or you could stack them, as they had at the end of the chalet village and across the road at the Aussie SF facility, Camp Russell, to create barracks units. T walls surrounded the DFAC, with one area designated as a memorial site. The names of the fallen were painted on the wall, much like the Vietnam Memorial in Washington, DC, along with the flags of Australia, the United States, Slovakia, and the Netherlands. Later additions to that wall memorial would come, along with the names of soldiers I had worked alongside.

The MNBTK memorial wall, ANZAC Day 2012

The Windmill sported a nice camouflage-covered deck along an exterior wall-painted with a typical euro graffiti-like design, with orange being the dominant color. This was the hangout for the remaining Dutch personnel on MNBTK and the site of my afternoon coffee break with my Dutch European Police, EUPOL for short, colleagues. They were such a civilized bunch of guys and tall too. Behind the Windmill was a large, covered outdoor recreation facility where Ping-Pong could be played and rugby, both league and union, could be enjoyed on the *tele*. This was the Australian USO-style area known as Poppy's. It was a bit of an inside joke as to whether it referred to an old man's nickname or the opium poppy that covered the land around the base. There was another multi-bomb-proofed container building just on the other side of the outdoor facility that completed Poppy's. It housed a lounge with several televisions, reading material, and a main source for access to coffee machines that could produce café lattes when the DFAC was closed. We may have been in the middle of nowhere, but the modern Western armed forces have certain needs that must be met if they are to stay ten-plus years in such remote areas. More conveniences would arrive over the following year that would highlight the massive spending in Afghanistan for troop comforts, which drove the $10-million-a-month price tag for our efforts there. It all had a feeling of the old British Raj of the 1700s in neighboring India.

Just beyond Poppy's, across a dirt road that would turn to mud during the winter if it wasn't frozen, was the Camp Holland headquarters area. Letters instead of numbers designated the chalets there. The area was fenced off and was accessible only if you had the combination to the lock on one of the several doors that accessed the area. The combination lock on the main entrance was notorious for failing on a regular basis. The combination was different for each gate, and it seemed the periodic changes to the combinations would occur during a time when you were away from the base, so you would return with the frustration of not being able to enter your work area unassisted. All civilians on the base had to wear identification badges around their necks that showed the level of access they were allowed to have. You could easily walk to any of the camps that comprised MNBTK, including the Afghan Army and Afghan Special Ops brigades located on MNBTK. The close proximity of those camps created some anxious times when the green-on-blue shootings started to rise in 2012.

Given the grid layout of the base, it didn't take long to know where you needed to go for any given thing. Having only one vehicle made staying in shape easy, for on any given day, you could easily walk five miles in the course of your work and not even notice it. The day would take on a rhythm, beginning with the opening of the DFAC at 0530 as the sunrise would backlight the mountains to our southeast, being ready to roll out the front gate by 0730, and then returning to writing reports coupled with a series of meetings that could push the day well into the night. I began to manage my day around all the work that needed to be accomplished, sliding workouts, power naps, and feedings into time slots that would open up.

This little city of foreigners plopped down in one of the most remote areas of Afghanistan had a rhythm and pulse such that those looking upon it from the other side of the wall could only shake their heads. We operated on a 24/7 schedule to accomplish our goals within a tour, which could be as short as six months, and then pass our assignments off to another. Outside the wall, the locals would talk about Alexander the Great as if he had traveled through just last week.

The Uruzgan Rule of Law Mix: EUPOL, UPRT, TF 66, AFP, Tim, and the Bee Charmer

"What are you doing about the rule of law, Tim?" The frustration on the face of the man across from me was obvious. "That's what Col. Creighton said to me just yesterday, Jeff." I felt the man's frustration. I had been on MNBTK just one day, and I could see the efforts in that area were disjointed, spread over several different organizations, and the commanding officer of Combined Team Uruzgan was chewing this retired FBI investigator's rear end off concerning an area for which he wasn't accountable. Tim was a police advisor embedded with the US military unit that was supposedly mentoring the local Afghan National Police (ANP). Tim didn't have an answer for him because there was little in Tim's position he could do concerning that overall subject. The ANP were formed as a national police force under the former communist regime. Rural Afghanistan had never had a local police force. When a crime had been committed in the past, the tribal elders would designate a few of the local men to go and bring the alleged offender to them for trial. After the trial, based on reconciliation rather than punishment, those men would go back to their fields, and in most cases the accused paid compensation to the victim's family. In severe crimes, the young girls of the accused man's family paid the price as "baad." In cases of murder, the accused may even be banished from the community, which in times past would be the equivalent of a death sentence, for no one survived out here without family ties. However, even in those cases, it was considered a great virtue of the victimized family to forgive the murderer and welcome him back. Reconciliation is what Afghans of the Pashtu regions strive to do.

In our eagerness to create civil society with government institutions, we reconstituted the ANP across Afghanistan and established local commands in the rural regions. The problem was they weren't educated as police officers to "protect and serve" the community. They were trained by our military as a paramilitary organization to augment the ANA, the Afghan National Army. At the time of my arrival, the commander of a US cavalry unit directly mentored the provincial chief of police (PCOP). The lieutenant colonel assigned the task was so out of touch with the role of a policing unit within a criminal justice system he had not brought Tim along with him to advise the PCOP. There was an Australian Federal Police mentoring unit and a European

Union Police (EUPOL) advisor team on the base that were also kept away from the PCOP. Tim and the other advisor teams did have access to the police training center on the base, and the Australian SF Task Force 66 worked directly with the rapid-response unit of the ANP, but none worked directly with the then PCOP, Juma Gul. Tim was on his way home for a well-deserved rest, and I could see that, like Iraq, a brief education of the military command on the status of the situation was needed. It didn't help that Tim's counterpart, working with the US troops in Deh Rawud, didn't see any problem with letting the police handle the complaints of the citizens rather than mentoring them to pass things on to the local prosecutor for disposition. The Dutch had just completed a comprehensive report concerning Uruzgan and its governance capabilities. One statistic stood out for me. Less than sixty major crimes had made their way into the local court system from March 2009 through March 2010, roughly the Afghan calendar year. That showed a near complete disconnect between the police and the rest of the criminal justice system, particularly between the police and prosecutor's office. I coupled this report with several academic papers, concerning the adverse effects on the criminal justice system of creating a paramilitary police force generally and the US military's specific efforts to do so, setting out the near impossibility to reverse the force into one that can become a community police force. This in effect placed the lack of movement in the rule of law area squarely at the feet of the US military's approach to mentoring the ANP. The report laid out a plan to bring together all the efforts being made amongst all the mentoring units, to create a synergy from those separate efforts that would hopefully coalesce out in the legal community of Uruzgan. Having the problem laid at the feet of the US military was greeted with silence. Tim never heard from Col. Creighton again on the issue. I was left with the struggle of how to bring the players together. All were under separate commands and had separate mission objectives. I had some coalition building of my own to accomplish.

One work chalet over from me sat the two remaining offices of the Dutch PRT EUPOL contingent. There was also a Dutch development office that remained to oversee the closeout of some major Dutch projects. In addition to some road projects, the Dutch had committed to the completion of the airport and the building of a civilian air terminal, vital projects for such an isolated area as Uruzgan. A tall, lanky Ping-Pong-playing woman, by the name of Wiesje, was the Dutch development officer in charge of those projects. She sported a great sense of ironic humor that kept us focused and on our toes.

Walking the well-worn path between chalets, I found the door of an office with the circle of stars symbol of the European Union stuck on the door. In the center of the circle of stars was the acronym EUPOL. Opening the door for the first time, I was transported into that EURO zone of good conversation accompanied by a good cup of coffee. Jan, Wilhem, Jos, Theo, and Johannes greeted me with warm smiles and good humor. Jan was working closely with the judges and prosecutors while the others worked with the police investigators. It was the start of a good professional relationship and, better yet, a warm friendship. It was clear from the beginning they were also frustrated with the lack of contact with the PCOP and the lack of efforts made toward creating a community policing force. Jan, who sported a slim, jawline, gray beard like mine, took me over to meet the Australian Federal Police mentoring unit on MNBTK. There I met Keith, who had been part of the team that stood up the Provincial Police Training Center just outside Camp Holland but still within MNBTK. Due to the policy of his government, they weren't allowed to travel outside of the MNBTK perimeter in their mentoring efforts. After a brief conversation with him, it was clear that my first order of business was to be a coordinator of the efforts of both of these extremely competent organizations toward an overarching goal of establishing a community-based criminal justice system in Uruzgan, EUPOL with their outside capability building on the inside training provided by the AFP.

Jos, me, Michael, Theo, and Wilhem

Theo and Tim at the PGOV's residence inside the compound

Right after that, we walked down to what was known as the PRT House to meet the provincial chief judge Malavi Mohammad Jan. He and I would become dear friends, sharing personal thoughts about our families and our hopes for the future. We dared to trust each other and reaped the rewards of that trust. However, on this day I was Jan's guest, and my only inquiry concerned the ability of the Uruzgan judges to attend a two-week judicial training course being held in Kandahar. The whirlwind was starting quickly. I had only been on the ground about thirty hours.

The following week resulted in meetings with the TF 66, Australian Special Forces Unit, Rule of Law Cell, which was a unique focus for an SF unit. The US Special Forces had nothing like it across the base at Camp Ripley. However, they were so far out in the wilderness, their rule of law focus had to remain on using the tribal elders as a hybrid source of prosecution and judgment. TF 66 had a special mandate to stand up the ANP quick reaction force and coordinate that force with Office of the Prosecutor of Political Crimes, a.k.a. the National Defense and Security prosecutor or NDS for short. Essentially, they were focused on developing the capacity to prosecute the Taliban wherever possible. A good idea, except it was so focused on insurgency crimes that it did nothing to either develop a criminal justice system or improve the legal system for the entire region. Since the police are the main contact point citizens are most likely to encounter, it was a missed opportunity to create a ground-level acceptance of the Afghan government. This expanded effort was outside of their mandate, so I set up some time with their commanding officer to seek his advice and assistance to incorporate what they were doing into a broader effort. I must say that not only did he get behind it, but this unit would be responsible for bringing in what I considered the crown jewel of the available training efforts, EUPOL's Cooperation of Police and Prosecutors course, COPP. It hadn't been developed in December 2010, so our own EUPOL contingent didn't have it available, and it wouldn't become so until after they had left MNBTK in April 2011. When it did become available, Shane, a fiery redheaded Aussie Special Forces soldier who had been in and out of Uruzgan several times, went to great lengths to get the program to MNBTK. Traveling multiple times to the EUPOL headquarters in Kabul and back again, it seemed by his sheer will he brought the COPP program to Tarin Kowt. He would leave it to my AusAID colleagues and me to figure out the logistical nightmare of finding classrooms, food, and lodging. I would comment many times to him that I didn't know whether to kiss him or kill him. He was also instrumental in bringing the multiple law enforcement professionals from the group together to provide training for Uruzgan prosecutors, judges and police in crime scene investigations.

Shane working his *CSI* magic with, left to right, Col. Hanif, Prosecutor Latif, Chief Prosecutor Mustafa, and Deh Rawud Prosecutor Shah Mohammad eagerly engaged

Uruzgan PRT was blessed with one such professional who was with a state of Maryland sheriff's office. Clay was a USN Reserve master-at-arms petty officer, first class. He was an example of those who stepped forward, above and beyond their regular duties, adding their civilian expertise to our efforts. Again, he extended our training reach out into the community outside the walls that kept the AFP confined. Simple mentoring efforts while on other missions outside the wire to bring the prosecutors and the police together in the community proved invaluable in the long run, even if in a particular case they seemed to fall short. It was the direction, a systematic approach to criminal justice, he was pointing them in that mattered.

Clay instructing prosecutors on crime scene investigations

The Australian civilian contingent of the PRT had an agency embedded with it called Australian Aid (AusAID) whose US counterpart was the United States Agency for International Development (USAID). The Aussies had no rule of law mentor position equivalent to that of the US State Department, but they did have a law and justice position. In that position, I would meet a lady by the name of Richelle. She was a hidden jewel. She could charm honey from a bee. Her ability to disarm the stoic Pashtu males came in handy. She was able to get most all the data we needed, which could be a struggle, with just a smile and a quick, "I'm sure that information would be easy to find" statement. She understood and embraced my systematic approach to the justice system, and through her efforts, AusAID would bring the funding to place a public defender in Tarin Kowt after USAID denied my request. Uruzgan was not a key terrain, according to the US policy makers, and as such we didn't qualify for the funding to get the program started. The two of us came to see that the best path to stability and growth of the justice sector in Uruzgan was to focus on how the population engaged "justice providers" in the province, and then mentor the entire group we had access to. We set out a roadmap with the goal of creating a working relationship between all of the Afghan justice sector actors that were interactive and then augment that with an education framework of dispute resolution within the Hanifi sharia, and thereby the Afghan Constitution, gearing it toward each group. This meant a focus on traditional *shura* dispute resolution, which at the time was controversial and in many coalition quarters actively opposed. The lynch pin of the approach was to have each justice group, both formal and informal, interact with the others. This meant encouraging them to discuss among themselves the win-win concept of communicating with each other and thereby creating consensus between them as to how to move forward. USAID had a program that fit the bill for the tribal elders, entitled Rule of Law-Informal (ROL-I) training, while another US-funded program through the Justice Sector Support Program (JSSP) was perfect for the formal sector. Getting those programs to Uruzgan wouldn't be easy. Our role on the Afghan side was to develop the relationships that would open up the trust between the justice sector actors to create the synergies necessary for a functioning criminal justice sector. It was a systematic community approach that would benefit all. It is critical to understand that for these justice sector actors, their tribal affiliations influenced how they worked together. Some were more closely tied to the Taliban than others. All the judges were outside of the Popalzai tribe, which was the tribal affiliation of Matiullah Khan, the local strongman who held the key to security and would later become PCOP. Richelle would be key in bringing the money in from Australia to fund the ROL-I program while I lobbied to break the JSSP program free from the Kandahar/Kabul-centric thinking to a mobile education program. The logistics of housing the instructors and transporting them to the training sites in Tarin Kowt would be a huge challenge. The willingness of the military to assist in any way collided with the contract rules concerning who could be fed at our DFAC and who could be housed within MNBTK, especially when green-on-blue shooting incidents increased in mid-2012. The mentality that we needed to bring our risk level to near zero conflicted with our mission to get the justice sector trained and functioning.

The success that the rule of law efforts made in the short period of time we had would be the result of a team of people who came together as individuals, crossing command lines, in an effort to put together a criminal justice system in Uruzgan. I was a conductor of sorts. I had no authority to demand anything from any of the organizations involved. I spent the time laying out my systematic approach and asking where they felt their efforts fell within that approach. Then I worked at bringing them all together to coordinate the separate efforts. We found ways to assist each other where we could, not because we were ordered to but because we all believed in the mission. Those in law enforcement and criminal justice in the Western world know that a safe community with equal access to justice is the cornerstone of a stable society. Society in rural Afghanistan had been by rule of violent tribal politics, and not the law, for so long it was imperative that the citizens could find a sense of stable justice if this civil war were ever to draw to a close.

Public defender and the bee charmer

The people I would work with over the next two and half years were not only professional but also great people who made the harsh work environment enjoyable. Key among them were the "bee charmer" and Jan from EUPOL, who I wish could have been there those last six months to see our ideas working in the Uruzgan justice sector community without us.

"The Only Thing Worth Dying For?"

"Why are the Taliban fighting so hard for this piece of rock, Uruzgan?" was the question Steve, a.k.a. "Banger," kept asking me as he dealt out the cards for what would become a regular Saturday evening of Five Hundred with our Aussie colleagues. A tough, now inactive USMC sergeant who was the bearded CTU Human Terrain Team director, Banger would often roam the countryside with the troops, engaging locals. Put him in a turban and local clothing, and he would blend into the crowd. It was a question we both wanted answered.

Weeks had passed, and I was getting settled in. Jan from EUPOL had been taking me with him to the primary court, prosecutor's office, prison, and the Ministry of Justice office in Tarin Kowt. The weather had turned cold, and each small office we went into had a wood-burning stove made out of a fifty-five-gallon steel drum sitting upon a brick foundation and a stove pipe made of steel ducting that would rise up about three to five feet and then take a hard ninety-degree turn to be vented through the nearest window. These offices were located within walking distance of the PGOV's compound, which was one of two well-fortified areas in the Tarin Kowt, the other being the ANP headquarters just a short but tense fifteen-minute walk away. Since most of the PRT's efforts were focused at the PGOV's compound, Jos and Wilhem would drive in with one of EUPOL's armored Mercedes-Benz SUVs tucked between Aussie Bushmaster vehicles, their version of the MRAP, where Jan and I rode. They would peel off as we passed the road leading into the ANP headquarters.

Jan and I would then walk from the PGOV's compound to the different offices along with an escort of several Aussie "Diggers," the affectionate name given to the Australian enlisted ranks during the

Battle of Gallipoli during WWI. This procedure was so high risk that it would be discontinued in 2012.

The process of getting us there would begin the night before with a movement briefing with the Australian "Other Government Agencies" Platoon, or OGA for short. There were usually several missions going out to many locations throughout the Tarin Kowt bowl region. The routes were very predictable, and that raised the IED risk. Engineers, with their route clearance duties, were constantly clearing the routes to keep us safe. We would rally outside the back gate of the CTU/PRT compound about 0730 hours for an additional briefing and final weather clearance. We could not leave the base in bad weather if the distance we were traveling required a helicopter medical evacuation, MEDIVAC, as the primary return of wounded in case of an IED. This rarely affected travel into Tarin Kowt City. The Australian MRAP is a unique vehicle. Longer than most US MRAPs, it had a much smoother ride, though you had to be a mountain goat to climb up into the vehicle. Painted in camouflage, they all had names or phrases painted on the side, like "Gone Fishin'" or other humorous titles, much the same way armored units did in Vietnam and in WWII. The first step on a "Bushie" is so high you have to bend your leg as much as possible and lift as high as you can to reach the handhold.

The best strategy to enter the vehicle while weighed down with body armor was to grab the handhold just outside the door and the one on the inside of the open door before lifting your leg up so you could pull yourself up into the vehicle. Once in, you sat on one of the rather comfortable seats facing inboard and strapped yourself in. The space was crowded but adequate. They had a remote machine gun mounted on the roof between the driver and the gunner who sat next to him. There was a gunner's hatch at the rear on the portside of the vehicle, where the rear gunner stood upon his seat, looking out. The temperature inside coincided with the temperature outside—cold in the winter and hot and dusty in the summer. Sure the vehicle had heating and air-conditioning, but with the open hatches, it tended to be moderated and not alleviated.

Once we were ready to roll the convoy of about three to four vehicles, depending on the number of persons going out to meeting, we would head usually out the front gate of MNBTK and straight into the outskirts of Tarin Kowt City that had grown almost right up to the gate. The living compound of the local warlord sat about two hundred meters directly across from the main gate. It was a symbiotic relationship that Matiullah Khan was keen to maintain. You could see out the front window of the Bushie, and after about a mile, we would turn onto the main highway that connected Tarin Kowt to Kandahar. This portion had been paved some years earlier, and there was a constant flurry of activity along the road into the center of the city. We would come up to the main roundabout, which was very congested. All along the way, you could see the many different, and some indifferent, looks from the population. Many were unmistakably hostile. Approaching the PGOV's compound, you could see an armed checkpoint with concertina wire scattered across the roadway between it and the edge of the wall as the only barrier to entering through the archway leading into the compound. Once inside, we dismounted, and I observed what from the outside looked to be one compound but was really two separated compounds. We parked just inside the main wall next to an old white building that was used as the deputy governor's compound and administration building. A new building was being built across a large, open space about two hundred meters away. People were milling about, some heading to work on the new administration building, while others lined the southern wall of the building we were next to, catching the warmth of the sun. The PGOV's home and office were inside another walled area, guarded by a strong steel drop bar and several armed guards. I walked down to the main gate looking out over the mountains in the distance.

A large crowd had gathered by the checkpoint we had passed while coming in. They were waiting to be let into the compound to go to work or petition the PGOV for one thing or another. As I stood there looking, I realized I made a nice target for a sniper and that if the Taliban wanted to, they could breach this front gate area very easily. That supposition would be tested in July 2011.

Jan and the Diggers had gotten ready, so it was time to step out. Our first stop would be the prosecutor's office. Being the only one without a weapon, I stepped into the middle of the formation as we walked out of the front gate and past the awaiting crowd. We made a hard left onto the first road past the checkpoint. Again, walls lined both sides of the street, but you could see over them into the boys' school on our left and the main mosque on our right. As we walked down this dirt road, the distinct smell of human urine and feces permeated my nostrils. You could see people squatting down and obviously relieving themselves in the dirt. Others were walking around with shovels, picking up feces. This was the local latrine. There were several small, permanent latrine structures at the end of the street, but at this time they were not functional other than as a more private relief area.

Sanitation workers in the alley, December 2010

It was a sanitation project that was being worked on with some rather bumbling results. Specifically, the Australians had built a water-treatment facility outside of Tarin Kowt for about one million AUSD. The latrines in the city were to be hooked up to multiple septic structures. They purchased a very large septic truck that was to be used to suck out the sewage in the septic structures. The septic structures were not prefabricated tanks. They were the traditional holes dug into the ground and lined with brick. The problem with all of this was the truck's suction ability far exceeded the strength of the septic structures. Any attempt to suck out the waste led to the collapse of the septic structure itself. Even more frustratingly comical was the fact that the mayor of Tarin Kowt was receiving gas for the truck, which was observed to be dismantled in several pieces in the yard next to his office. When the Australians attempted to retrieve the truck, it "disappeared" for months. The effort to retrieve the truck was the bane of Luke, the head of AusAID at UPRT at the time. The mere mention of the truck would set him off on a response full of the favorite Aussie adjective, "fuck."

"Shit Alley" as viewed on a return trip to the
PGOV compound, December 2012

"Shit Alley," as it was affectionately called by the troops, avoided the market street and therefore was the safe way from the PGOV's compound to courts, police headquarters, and prosecutor offices. This separation from the PGOV's compound and these other vital components of local governance was not only physical but also a real fault line in how the local politics played out. The constant refrain from the provincial chief judge Malavi Mohammad Jan was that those outsiders who held the position of provincial governor came only to steal from the people of Uruzgan.

Turning left, we walked just about twenty meters down the road to the prosecutor's office on the right-hand side. Nothing special marked the door, though the wall that surrounded the building, rather house, was marked in paint as the prosecutor's office. Like most structures along the road, it had a wall about fifteen feet high around it, with the sides and back being shared by the building on the other side of the wall. Stepping off the street and through the metal door in the wall, I came upon an unusual scene. Like most Afghan buildings, the prosecutor's building sat about twenty feet from the wall in front and about half that on the sides. Now to the left of the door, the earth rose up, and I could see that there was a small irrigation stream flowing through that side of the compound. Placed directly in front of the building was the shell of an automobile that was curiously half-buried, as if it had been the victim of a mudslide.

The small one-level building had an open hallway dividing the two halves of the structure. There were two doors on either side of the hall, rusted and covered with a heavy blanket to help insulate the metal from the cold. No one was there, so Jan pulled out his trusty, well-used cell phone and began what I would soon learn was his usual routine of having to chase down this particular prosecutor, Mahmud, to attend an already scheduled meeting.

While he did that, I sat out on the ground near the irrigation stream. I was learning the joys of the high-altitude sun on a cold winter day as I looked over the top of the wall at the people walking by. The caretaker of the grounds, an older, white, bearded man, sat across from me doing the same. He was curiously looking me over while he sat casually cross-legged and slumped over, with his hands folded across his lap. Unlike in Iraq, women were conspicuously absent from the hustle and bustle of people walking the street on the other side of the wall. They weren't totally absent but were rare.

Tarin Kowt is a city of no more than forty thousand people. Most of the faces of the residents that I saw were Pashtu and not the oriental-looking Hazaran. They carry the Chinese gene, as Genghis Khan slaughtered all the males of the tribe and replaced them with his own men. Though this province was originally "Hazaragan," the Hazaran tribe was forced by the Pashtu to the northeastern area known as Khas Uruzgan and the northern area of Uruzgan, known as Day Kundi, which is now a province of its own. The Hazaran are a fierce group, and in Uruzgan there were constant clashes between the two sects. The Hazaran are also of the Shia sect of Islam, which made them heretics in the eyes of the Hanifi Sunni sect and therefore absolutely hated by the Wahhabist Taliban. The Taliban would throw them into prison for failing to have a beard. Oriental men have great difficulty in doing so, and as a result, many spent years in prison until some semblance of a beard sprouted. I never met a Hazaran who couldn't speak English at a basic level, and the areas under their control had a strong education ethic. The scene on this street in Tarin Kowt was mostly one of bearded men walking with their hands carried in the traditional posture behind them and a slight lean forward. The women who were about traveled in groups with an elderly female dressed in black or with a male, usually a child, with them. Except for the very old with the traditional black garb covering all but their faces, they were covered in burkas. Young girls and boys were seen all the time, but as soon as a girl started to show signs of puberty, she was covered.

Children of women attending JSSP training

Though covered, personal expression is seen at the ankle level

The burka, a symbol in the West of all that is wrong with Afghanistan's treatment of women, is worn in Uruzgan as protection. Sure, protection from ignorant responses from the males and of harsh results of outdated, backward norms, but much-needed protection nonetheless. The honor of the family, and therefore the honor of the males in that family, is held in many ways by the women of the family.

41

Violation of that honor falls on a woman, even if unintentional or by the act of another, such as rape. In Western nations, the thought that a woman brings the violent act of rape upon herself was only recently, in cultural terms, discarded. Rape shield laws protecting rape victims from questioning them about their past sexual behavior weren't in place across the entire United States until the early 1980s. However, this idea still flourishes in Central Asia and the Indian subcontinent with terrible consequences. A woman's own family will kill her to save the family's honor. Therefore, the burka is the first line of defense in any questioning of a woman's honor in Uruzgan. Women are treated in ways much like a commodity or chattel in Uruzgan, much the same way they were viewed under Western laws well into the 1600s, even 1700s. If a wrong demands money damages, then the wrongdoer will often give a female child to satisfy the debt. It is known as baad and is practiced throughout the region. Baad is the name for the price one demands as the price for having someone's daughter in marriage. Every area has a known price for a bride. So when money damages are to be paid in this subsistence region, a daughter can be given over instead. It is also seen, erroneously in most cases, as a way to reconcile the two families and create a larger family group. Sadly, it most often creates nothing more than a slave in the new household. So the question is, are the damages the price of one bride, a half of a bride, or two brides? The answer to those questions will determine the age or number of the women being offered to settle the claim for damages. This attitude toward women exists while pedophilia acts by men against young boys and sex between men, who may have more than one wife, is common with little public outrage at all. In fact, they consider homosexuality as a sin under Islam but don't see the "man sex" as such because they "don't love" each other. As confusing as that sounds, I couldn't wonder if this was the behavior of the Macedonian invaders under Alexander the Great trapped in a time warp. History is full of stories of such behavior from the Macedonians and Greeks. Though MMJ, the chief judge, would constantly preach against those acts, I would be involved in situations time and again where an ANP checkpoint commander was under investigation for not only having sex with a young boy but murdering him afterward—often to no avail. It was that common. Those were things I would come to learn more about personally, but on this day, Jan and I left the prosecutor's office to walk ten more minutes up the road to the primary court to meet with that court's colorful chief judge, Haji Abdul Wahid Acheckzai.

Unlike walking the streets of Tarmiyah in Iraq, where we walked the market street to get to my meetings, in Tarin Kowt we avoided the market street. It was just too dangerous to walk through with my small group. The roadway we walked had no shops, and the people on the sidewalks would look at you with scowls. Children kept their distance, and those walking in the street stayed clear. Several weeks later while making this same walk, that abruptly changed when a young man of about fourteen or fifteen years old slipped between two of the Diggers and quickly walked up to me. I felt terror. I had let myself relax, and the moment I had to react to a suicide bomber had passed in the blink of an eye. It was a rookie mistake, and I was no rookie.

Walking the street in Tarin Kowt into the ANP compound area

It happened so fast, but I was fortunate because he just smiled directly in my face and just as quickly walked away. I had just been tagged. Tagging was a dry run made to see if you were vulnerable to a suicide attack, and we were. Shortly thereafter, I received an intelligence report from EUPOL warning me that a specific death threat against me had been uncovered. I had a long talk with my Diggers, shared the report, and then placed the report in the back pocket of my moleskin notebook to be pulled out whenever my PSD detail changed personnel. No one ever got through again.

Tough security on the road

Unfortunately, one young man paid with his life when he failed to heed the warning to stop his motorcycle as he quickly approached us. Even more unfortunate, it was a cousin of the provincial Ministry of Justice (MOJ) interim director who Richelle and I were meeting with at the time. It was a tough spot our soldiers were in, having to make such decisions in a split second. However, failure to do so caused the death of two American officers and the interpreter when no one reacted to him shouting, "Shoot him, someone! Shoot him!" as a young man quickly penetrated the group of soldiers outside the ANP substation just one hundred meters from the civil prosecutor's office our group visited on a regular basis. It's a moment of disbelief that it is actually happening, as in Chora when a young man dressed in white, mumbling prayers, waited next to a wall for my Australian colleague Dave and USMC Captain Brad to walk by. He slipped in behind a soldier, and even with another looking in disbelief at the event, it was too late. The only thing that saved Dave was the fact the young man stumbled as he detonated the bomb, aiming most of the blast into the ground. This caused most of the ball bearings and other shrapnel to blow into the ground and then ricochet upward, minimizing the penetration. The concussion, however, shattered all the bones in his legs and arms and delivered a concussive injury to his brain. He lived, but both he and Captain Brad have a long road to recovery.

Jan made contact with the primary court chief judge, so we headed out to meet him. We turned right out of the prosecutor's office compound to walk the next hundred yards of this road before turning left at the ANP checkpoint, which blocked access to the road leading another fifty yards toward several government buildings and the ANP headquarters. That road made a hard ninety-degree turn and then dead-ended, so to speak, about another fifty yards into a large HESCO barrier. The road continued on the other side, but for now we were within a secured area that held a large compound on the left side of the road that housed the ANP barracks and HQ. On the right side of the road, behind walls, of course, were four buildings that the Dutch had built as homes to attract judges to the area. I never got the full story, but let's just say things didn't work out as the Dutch had anticipated. This would be true of another rather large Dutch project, a road meant to connect the city of Tarin Kowt with the city of Chora. However, I'll save that story for later. Three of the houses were occupied by the ANP for officer quarters and to house the internal investigations prosecutor known as a military prosecutor, Mohamad Zai Khan. I would come to learn that he was a very proud man and well educated. It was well known that women of the Mohamadzai tribe were strong and insisted that their husbands be educated. The remaining building had been turned into the primary court with administrative offices and living quarters for the three judges that worked there. All that was squeezed into a building containing two ten-foot by twelve-foot rooms, two ten-foot by ten-foot rooms, and a ten-foot by ten-foot entry hall that led to the other rooms. There were gardens planted in the front and rear of the compound, which was quite common with any structure whose grounds could maintain a home garden. There was another structure along the back wall that contained two ten-foot by ten-foot rooms and a latrine. There was no running water, just a pump in the middle of the back garden. In some places, a hose would be attached, and they would pump the water to a cistern on the roof, and that would provide the running water in the building.

Upon entering the structure, Jan was warmly greeted by Acheckzai, a robust man standing about five nine, sporting the distinct potbelly created by a plentiful amount of the delicious flat bread and mutton that graced many older men in Uruzgan with a little wealthier position in life. He was clearly pleased to see Jan as he guided us back into the office to the right on the entry, which led into his personal quarters that he shared with the two other judges. Jan introduced us, and he laughingly agreed with the observation of MMJ that we looked like brothers.

Haji Abdul Wahid Acheckzai

Entering the sleeping quarters, it was easy to see why Acheckzai was so glad to see Jan. There spread across the floors along the walls were, what I would call by their Danish name, "downers" (doo-ners), or in American English, we would call them comforters. Those down-filled, fluffy, warm winter covers were a Dutch royal blue. Stamped upon the field of blue was the crown of the Netherlands containing the Christian symbol of the cross. *How odd*, I thought, but I'm sure it never crossed their minds during the cold nights. We sat down on the floor to have some hot morning tea, a ritual I would repeat over and over on any visit to any place in Uruzgan.

It was their deeply held custom to provide refreshments for guests, regardless of the setting.

Haji Abdul Wahid, Jan, the author, Saba,
for Jan's farewell lunch

In the upper corner, just left of the door we had entered, was a television set tuned to a familiar station out of Jordan where women danced in traditional Arab belly-dancing outfits. For the men in this region, such a show was probably akin to pornography. I once saw several of our young male interpreters looking through a *GQ* magazine with the same delight as a fourteen-year-old male in the States might have looked through the women's lingerie section of a Sear's catalog in 1959. It's not possible to understate how far back in time, from a Western perspective, the rural Afghan culture sits in regards to male and female interaction. Papers have been written on this separation in the rural areas being the driver of the male sexual interaction and the pedophiliac behavior in the adult male population.

Acheckzai shared the building with two other judges, Abdul Razeeq and Abdul Kudos. Abdul Kudos was not from the area and would disappear for long periods of time. Abdul Razeeq would reveal he had been mujahedeen at the age of eighteen and a commander by age twenty. He had a bright smile of false teeth. The Russians had knocked out his original ones with a rifle butt. I would learn later that most of those with such fine teeth in Uruzgan were wearing dentures. Acheckzai was more the norm, several teeth missing and the rest very brown due to the poor diet and constant smoking. Over time, it was revealed to me that the primary court was very corrupt. Abdul Kudos's absent behavior was driven more by the fact that Abdul Razeeq was married to Acheckzai's daughter, and therefore they were in on the corruption together. The Afghans themselves would not reveal this relationship to me for another year. That is how closed to outsiders this culture is. On top of that, he had once been the mayor of Tarin Kowt but lost that position when Jan Mohamad Khan was replaced as PGOV. Acheckzai was given his judge position by the provincial chief judge MMJ. The interconnectedness of relationships was the foundation as to what drove the non-removal or removal of someone known to be corrupt. Once that relationship was revealed to me, I was able to have a productive conversation with the provincial chief judge MMJ. He made it clear that without the ability to bring someone to Uruzgan, he had to work as best he could with what he had. We often talked about making Acheckzai a better man, and I know he was pressuring him to be so. He would eventually reassign Abdul Razeeq up to Chora where his mujahedeen credentials would be a plus, but not until August 2013.

Over my two-plus years, I would get to know Acheckzai, and he would come to trust that I wanted the Afghans to work out their justice system for themselves. It moved to a point where he would ask my opinion on how to deal with certain perplexing issues. My favorite was the breakup of a business venture in the bazaar. It seems a pharmacist and a hardware dealer formed their business under the same roof. They had a partnership of sorts and were now breaking that relationship. They were able to come to agreement on all things except the thirteen kilos of raw opium in their building. "Now," the judge said to me, "under Afghan law, you can't hold, transport, or sell raw opium. So if I rule on how it is divided, have I not broken the law?" he queried. "How do I divide thirteen into equal parts?" I responded by saying that he had a difficult decision to make. What the law said and what the realities of Uruzgan were when it came to such things were at odds with each other. We laughed about how the court needed a new roof, and maybe the "administrative expenses" of the arbitration could solve the issue concerning an equal division of the opium. It was said in jest on my part, with the full understanding it was the reality.

Judge Haji Abdul Wahid Acheckzai at his court desk

Opium shaded everything in Uruzgan. However, opium aside, this same man would help put in place a court-tracking system through a USAID program that worked well, and the local police would come to him for a warrants before entering a house. It wasn't much of a formal affair. An ANP officer would just show up and make a statement that they had chased a man to a home and were waiting outside for a warrant to enter to arrest him. The judge would take a piece of paper, write down his authorization to enter, sign it, and then stamp it with the court seal. The process took about sixty seconds, but it happened. I would think of a "Judge Roy Bean" analogy many times when it came to Acheckzai and how he ran his primary court, corruption and all mixed into a Wild West blend of justice.

Over the next several months, Jan and I, along with the Australian legal officer from the CTU, would go to the primary court every Monday to observe the trials. I went to get a sense of how well they were going, and the Australian legal officer went to verify the fair treatment of the prisoners they had delivered into the system. The Afghan International Human Rights Commission (AIHRC) representative was also there. What I found absolutely fascinating was the activity of the judge on the days leading up to the trial. He would go to all the elders of the area and discuss what type of person the accused was and get their opinion on what the sentence should be. This more than anything was telling as to how the formal system really functioned. The group consensus was still the driving force. Their law, not "the law." The judge himself was an educated man but not educated by either the Sharia Law Faculty or the Secular Law Faculty in Kandahar or Kabul. His entire "law" education was his readings of the Koran, the Hadifas, and the USAID judicial training he had attended. He would often proclaim a defendant guilty based on the constitution of Afghanistan, which was a total misrepresentation of the codified law. It didn't really matter because the shuras held prior to the trial were probably more a factor than the law itself. Acheckzai would often ask me to build a court building with a large enough space to bring the elders into the trial process since his small office—with only his desk, one chair next to him for the prosecutor, and two sofas facing each other, separated by small tables for the tea—just wasn't large enough to accommodate the elders. Often they would be sitting outside the building when we came in, and they would select a spokesperson to come in and make a statement on behalf of the accused. Many of these cases involved the defendant having banned Taliban propaganda material on their cell phones or unregistered weapons. The propaganda materials would be subject to "a minor fine" under the law. It was a very subjective amount, and it was to be paid into a bank account held by the provincial court once they were released. This system was fraught with potential corruption, but it worked.

One case that stood out was that of a defendant found with one unregistered AK-47, several magazines, and hundreds of rounds of ammunition. He argued the usual, "My registered gun was taken by the Taliban, and that is why I have this one." The fine was usually based on the price of the AK-47. This one was rather new, but he argued it was old and not worth the 30,000 afghani fine. The judge pointed out that even if it was old, the fine took into account the extra magazines and ammunition. The word "afghani" is the same as the word "dollar." A citizen of Afghanistan is an Afghan, much the same as we in America are called Americans. However, the word "afghani" escaped many a military officer's lips when speaking about the people. I got tired of explaining this simple truth until I came up with the analogy that they wouldn't want Afghans to refer to us as dollars, "so please make the effort to show you know something of the culture." I often thought that this failure to learn the proper group name of the people was a subconscious need to not get to know them as people. It wasn't as rude or bad as "chink," "gook," or "Haji," but it did not go unnoticed.

Within a year these, trial-monitoring visits would end because the AIHRC representative was there, and we would meet with them on a regular basis. It was a way to transition over to total Afghan responsibility. In August 2012, General Abrams would roll into the Regional South Command (RC South) with his new plan for rule of law. Among his demands was that we monitor the trials of detainees. His judge advocate general's (JAG) officer just couldn't believe that we in Uruzgan had already transitioned that over to the Afghans in early 2012. It seemed no other PRTs in RC South had done that. It was a testimony of how well the roadmap Richelle and I had forwarded in early 2011 had been executed. It wasn't the only item on the general's list that we had already accomplished. The irony was RC South really didn't believe us, and we had to go back over all our reports sent to them, over a year's worth, to document our efforts. It was additional testimony of how disconnected our ISAF efforts were. However, it was reminiscent of a conversation I had a year and a half earlier with an army major at the Rule of Law Conference in Kabul. He was adamant that we had to follow the preset plan of establishing a specific number of prosecutors and courthouses in the districts in order to achieve success. I offered the observation that the Afghans didn't seem to want to push prosecutors or judges out to these rural regions. I said that maybe we should take another tack, such as meeting the rural Afghans where they were and mentor from a tribal justice position. He exploded with, "Do think you know more than General Petraeus?" My response, "In this arena, I believe I do," didn't go over well with him. That said, it did go over well with the civilian mentors in the field who were seeing the same reluctance on the part of the Afghans to embrace the system the coalition was pushing. We felt that the goal was worthy but not timely. We could get there but not anytime soon; it was a generation away. As a Vietnam veteran who was there during the "Vietnamization" of the conflict, I could see history repeating itself. In fact, I could see that the lessons of Vietnam had been lost by the military along the way. I would see the belief on the part of the military that the American people and the Afghans would want us in Afghanistan at this level for a long time. You had to buy into that because, by definition, counterinsurgency took twenty-seven years to win. That was contrary to the reality of what our US economy could absorb and the stated 2014 withdrawal timeline for most US forces. It also would fly in the face of some of the first words out of the Afghan president Ashraf Ghani's mouth in his September 25, 2014 inauguration speech, where he spoke of the goal of having no foreign fighters in Afghanistan. The Western news reports labeled that as a reference to the foreign Islamist fighters going into Syria and Iraq, but I'm not so sure he didn't mean all foreign troops, including the ISAF/NATO forces.

This discussion did not go unnoticed. Shortly thereafter came the directive of focusing on "sustainable stability," which translated to the dreaded phrase, "Afghan good enough." It was déjà vu all over again because that language had been used in my last months in Iraq. There came a growing acceptance that a hybrid model of governance and rule of law would be the structure of stability in rural Afghanistan. Maybe it was my age, or how I grew up in a rural environment that was transitioning to a suburban environment, but I saw this hybrid model being a natural steppingstone to a more formally structured future. Had we not gone through such a phase in our own country? I knew informal dispute resolution that valued the offender as a member of the community was part of our past. At age fourteen, I committed a criminal offense that would today land a young person before a judge, but back in 1964 put me in a room with the local police and fire chiefs, along with my mom. It was the mainstream in rural Afghanistan today and will remain so for the immediate future, so working with it and not against it seemed to be the sane choice. However, that went against those who wanted to build a nation based on modern Western ideals.

Getting back to Steve's question, I found part of the answer in the book by Eric Blehm titled *The Only Thing Worth Dying For*. Hamid Karzai, accompanied by a team of Green Berets, came to Uruzgan in November 2001 to meet with tribal militia and old mujahedeen leaders to forge a force against the Taliban. Those efforts led to the defeat of the Taliban and the surrender of the city of Kandahar. Tarin Kowt, Uruzgan, was ground zero in a culture where symbolism mattered.

With all the woes we lamented about how corrupt and immoral the culture here seemed to us, it was a culture struggling to move forward. Many good Americans had died to wrestle this land from the Taliban, whose spiritual leader Mullah Omar had grown up in Deh Rawud, which sat just west of Tarin Kowt. Acheckzai's own brother, a Taliban, would later be killed in a night raid by Australian forces. The head of the provincial court of appeals civil division, Taj Mohammad, was the provincial chief judge under the Taliban. His own son would later set the IED that would take his life while at prayer at the city's mosque, because Taj stayed on under GIRoA. The present chief judge MMJ was a member of the Tohki tribe, a subtribe of the Ghilzai driven to the Taliban after Jan Mohammad Khan (JMK) had so brutally suppressed them. He had a very close relationship to Hamid Karzai. I would learn later that it came from his support to Karzai when he brought the Green Berets to Tarin Kowt. That alliance made him the constant target of the Taliban. This was a minefield of cross relationships that went on under our noses, without giving a thought about rigid alliances but fully aware of keeping options open. Tribal, kinship, and business relationships were the governing ethos of this region, upon which the outside world was trying to impose a centralized democratic government. In the short term, it was doomed to failure. This concept of being a citizen of Afghanistan, instead of just an Afghan, is a Western idea. Getting

Afghans to work with Afghans was seemingly a constant goal. Watching Republicans and Democrats back home exhibit the same disconnected behavior was one of the real ironies of our efforts in Uruzgan.

However, leaving the US Congress out of the equation for now, the key to getting the job done in Uruzgan would be understanding the relationships at work. That would take time and a showing of a commitment to their way to bear fruit. What I'm saying is that I saw us in them. Therefore, I couldn't take any stand other than to develop their desire to create stability in their own way and then mentor from there, having faith that their reasoning would move them in a similar, not the same, direction we took so many years ago. We had to meet them where they were and where they were willing to go, in order to create the desired stability that could create the fertile ground where a modern Afghanistan could emerge from its long night of civil violence. I owed it to those who had died and to those who were going to die around me in this remote region of the world to give meaning to that sacrifice. I would find two Afghan heroes to create my own kinship network within their networks, to accomplish our goals in the justice sector and watch it spill over into governing Uruzgan itself. One was the provincial chief judge and spiritual leader Malavi Mohammad Jan. The other was an outsider, Dr. Abdul Gafar Stanikzai, the local director of the Afghan International Human Rights Commission, known by its acronym AIHRC.

Malavi Saab, Malavi Mohammad Jan Tohki, the Man Who Would Become the Most Powerful Man in Uruzgan

Malavi Mohammad Jan, pronounced Jaahn, much like the English John but pronouncing the O more like a soft long A, was a stately but humble man whose eyes would twinkle when he smiled. He claimed to be seventy-one years old, but given the average life expectancy for Afghan males is around forty-five to forty-eight, he may have been younger. He was a thin man whose smile was as captivating and warm as his hospitality. He would often clear his throat before he spoke and was always adjusting his dentures with a quick twitch of his mouth. He was a true Malavi, a highly religiously educated person, who always spoke in parables when it came to sensitive subjects. He spoke Pashtu, Dari, and Arabic. His grandfather sat as a senator in the parliament of King Mohamad Zai Shah while his father was the ambassador to Pakistan during the Russian occupation. MMJ, as we referred to him, had been a mujahedeen commander during the fight against the Russians. I was always escorting him onto the base for trainings and meetings. He once had me stop just as we were reaching the main gate of MNBTK. Directly west beyond the city of Tarin Kowt was a mountain range, part of the bowl that surrounded TK. Staring out at the range for several moments, he began to tell me of how he and his fighters would sit far up in those mountains as the Russians tried to blow them out with artillery. The look on his face and in his eyes told me he was far away in his mind, reliving days gone by. I could tell he longed for real peace. He was of the Tohki tribe, a subtribe of the Ghilzai, which is the largest tribe in Uruzgan but not in power. This fact would have a significant impact over the next years. The former Popalzai PGOV's, Jan Mohammad Khan, brutal suppression of the Ghilzai drove them into the Taliban camp. This made reconciliation talks difficult. The combination of MMJ's tribal affiliation and his position as a highly respected Malavi would help bridge those difficulties. The fact that he had the ear of President Hamid Karzai, a Popalzai, was also an indicator of his interconnections and importance. I never saw any young Afghan greet him with anything but a kiss of his hand, and the older ones with a hug and a kiss of the hand, from the provincial governor on down. This, more than anything, told me how respected he was. Though when I first arrived he had been marginalized locally and was under constant threat of attack, by July 2012 it was confessed to me by Dr. Stanikzai that MMJ had become the most powerful person in Uruzgan. "Not even the governor can resist him" was the statement made to me. Though in the winter of 2010 and 2011, that was far from the case. I didn't know it when I first met him, but he was working through the elder system to bring peace and unity to the region. He would reveal that to me over time as our friendship grew. His main stumbling block was MK, both because of his youthful hubris and the reluctance of the other tribes to work with MK, due to his favoritism toward the Popalzai and his past brutal behavior working for his uncle, former PGOV Jan Mohammad Khan. MMJ was operating totally under the radar of the PRT director, the CTU commander, and myself for a long time. Working closely with him aroused my suspicions that he was doing so because he often contradicted himself from week to week concerning the role of the formal courts and that of the many tribal shuras operating in the area.

Once I figured it out, I would use him to establish a strong functioning justice sector while he used me to give him the cover to do it his way. We were two "gray beards," men who embraced each other's belief in God and learned from each other as we worked for peace in the region. Getting to that understanding is a story of many meetings and subtle conversations using stories to get our meaning across. However, to understand the power of MMJ, you must know the story of Matiullah Khan (MK), Uruzgan's strongman by the time I arrived in 2010.

The author and Malavi Mohamad Jan, spiritual
leader and chief judge of Uruzgan Province

Matiullah Khan: Police Chief, Warlord, and the Security of Uruzgan

If you think power is tied only to guns and money, Matiullah Khan would qualify as the most powerful. However, in the world of the rural Pashtu, where real power comes from is the ability to bring consensus, he was operating at a huge deficit due to all who had reason to hate him. A tall, thin man in his late thirties who always seemed to be struggling with his health, MK, as we called him, was a classic Pashtu warlord. His thin black beard wrapped around his chiseled, angular face while his bright eyes, that missed nothing, gleamed from their sunken sockets. He was the nephew of and enforcer for Jan Mohammad Khan, the former PGOV. In that role, he acquired the reputation of a brutal man who would kill indiscriminately to bring a village or area under control. International human rights groups to this day stay focused on those times, while the local human rights director had found ways to accommodate the new MK into a greater picture. MK himself uses the reputation more today with a look or a nod of the head. That said, as the international forces leave, and with the Afghan elections possibly pushing the Popalzai out of power, MK's ability to survive will be tested. The Pashtu won't forget the need to avenge the deaths at his hand. The question will be, as in all conflict areas of the world, can reconciliation occur or will the spiral of conflict continue? It will clearly be a test for all of Uruzgan if transition can be peaceful.

Prior to JMK being PGOV, he was a prisoner of the Taliban, and MK was the man Hamid Karzai contacted, along with MMJ and others, with his plan to free the south from the Taliban, starting in Uruzgan. Acting on his uncle's behalf, he formed a militia group and then worked his way around to being useful, not only to Karzai but to the American Special Forces. He was brutal in his work for his uncle and that brutality would seal his fate in this land of blood feuds. However, when I had arrived in 2010 he had developed those relationships into a multimillion-dollar contract, estimated at $2.5 million a month, protecting the convoys that supplied MNBTK. He did this by forming his own highway patrol, a militia that later morphed into the Kandak-e-Amniat-e-Uruzgan (KAU). A Kandak is the name Afghan brigades are known by. This protection of the convoys gave him access to trucks that were used to transport items and people in and out of Uruzgan. Some were legal, others not. The opium paste harvested from Uruzgan's ten thousand hectares of poppy cultivation is a major source of income. A hectare of poppy can yield between eight to fifteen kilos of opium paste. At approximately $750 to $800 USD per kilo, the region produced a crop worth $7.5 million to $12 million just at the farm level. Now, he didn't control it all but enough of it to acquire influence far above his rank of a colonel in the ANP. In fact, his major rival for control of the opium was another police commander in the town of Dah Rawud, Omar Khan, a Noorazai, who was a miniature MK. They were rivals for some time, and in late 2012, MK moved Omar from Deh Rawud to Chora as a way to lessen his control over the opium trade in that region.

The CTU commander at the time of my arrival, a US Army colonel at the time, seemed to be infatuated with the fierce mountain Pashtu fighter image MK portrayed and made his way to MK's compound across the field from MNBTK's front gate whenever possible. Our special forces understand his effectiveness in dealing with the Taliban and therefore work with him. However, the former Dutch command was so outraged by him they pushed hard to get rid of him, to no avail. There is much written about MK in the world press, so a quick Google search will bring more information about this colorful figure if you so desire. However, the one observation I made of the man was his willingness to be patient and watch things develop around him and then be as subtle as possible in his actions. He went as far as creating own "peace and reconciliation" shura made up of elders in the Tarin Kowt bowl that competed with the courts in Uruzgan as a legitimate justice body. However, it told me he wanted his actions to have legitimacy of some sort, so one of the goals I set with MMJ was to bring that desire around to using the GIRoA judges and eventually the criminal justice system to provide that legitimacy. MK was very focused on consolidating his Uruzgan power base, which created the most effective PCOP of the three that held the position while I was there, he of course being the last. When he did take the position, one of the very first actions he took was to fill over one thousand positions that had been vacant "ghost" police positions. The previous PCOPs would collect the salaries for their own use. I'm sure MK used the positions for patronage jobs, but that was a productive use not aimed at lining his pockets. He needed the extra police-soldiers in his efforts to push the Taliban out. When he asked for the necessary weapons to arm them, Kabul replied those positions would not be continued. He traveled to Kabul with MMJ and other tribal elders, and not only did he return with the arms but extra positions to be filled.

Well into 2013, the Dutch were writing of their disgust of him even while they acknowledged that a broad group of tribal elders had embraced him and that he was one of two leaders in the south who was effectively countering the Taliban. (Afghan Analysts Network: Transition in Uruzgan (2): Power at the centre, by Deedee Derksen, 12 June 2013.) It seemed many in the international community wanted him replaced and someone else forced upon Uruzgan. I can only say that my conversations concerning him with many Uruzganis resulted in two main conclusions. They saw all outsiders coming to high office in

Uruzgan as only coming for their cut of the action and not really having the best interest of the people of Uruzgan at heart. The other was that they all understood how Uruzgan worked, and it was a closed society. MK may have had his issues, but they were Uruzgan's issues to deal with.

In the summer of 2011, Jan Mohamad Khan would be assassinated. With that came a power struggle between three young tribal leaders in Uruzgan: Mohammad Nabi Khan Tohki (MNKT), Mohammad Doad Khan (MDK), and Matiullah Khan. MDK and MNKT became very close and seemed to be working together. However, when the dust settled late in September 2011, Mohammad Doad Khan was dead, and Mohammad Nabi Khan Tohki had kowtowed to MK for the time being and quietly retreated into the seclusion of his tribal area. MK would replace the PCOP Fazi Amed Sherzad, a professional police commander who had only taken the post in May 2011. The fighting season closed out that year with Taliban fighters sending requests to him to be allowed to return safely to Pakistan before the mountains were snowed in. MK gave them three days. Shortly thereafter, PGOV Sharizad, who had arrived with me in December 2010, would announce he was departing too. January 2014 would arrive with MK's police force being seen by Uruzganis as good for the people, and Omar Khan, the former Norazai DCoP of Deh Rawud and MK's rival, being in charge of MK's personal bodyguard detail, with a gold-plated AK-47 and all. MK consolidated the power of the ANP and his KAU, all because MMJ, a man outside of the governmental political power structure, gathered tribal elders around him, made peace with MK, and paid a visit to President Hamid Karzai. So how did this all transpire?

MMJ Meets Jafer

My first meeting at the appeals court building with MMJ gave a snapshot of how justice was operating in Uruzgan. A formal court system was needed for insurgency crimes. Those who had taken that path were operating outside the traditional tribal arbitration system of the *jirga* or *shura*, depending on which language you were using, and therefore they wouldn't conform their behavior to abide by any elder's decisions. However, the large group of elders sitting on rugs in the warmth of the early February sun outside the building was there to discuss a long-running land dispute. Inside MMJ's small office sat

Haji Abdul Wahid, the primary court chief judge and former mayor of TK, Mulavi Taj Mohammad, the former chief judge under the Taliban government and now head of the civil division, Hamidullah, the head of the criminal division and local village elder, a representative of the Uruzgan Ullema, the religious council, the elders' committee, and MMJ. MMJ explained the group was from Deh Rawud and they had just shown up that morning. He knew they were coming at some time that week, but like all things in Uruzgan, Afghanistan, exact times were never guaranteed, much like it was in the 1600s and 1700s in America. (I told the meeting that the clock found in the home of George Washington only had an hour hand because that was the best time anyone could say. The minutes in between were not relevant.) Clearly in Uruzgan not even the day was relevant, for they were happy to allow us to conduct our meeting before turning their attention to the gathered group of elders. I insisted that they should conduct their business first, for it wouldn't be proper of me to take the time away from these elders who were waiting patiently outside after their long journey. MMJ smiled and said, "Your family raised you well." I told him I would enjoy watching the proceedings while accepting his hospitality of tea and sweets.

The judges of Uruzgan. Left to right: Taiub, MMJ, Hamidullah,
Haj Abdul Wahid, Abdul Razeeq, and Kudos.

I sat on the far right of the sofa where the round arm abutted up against the wall and the window looked out over the front of the appeals court compound. Several Afghan security persons were walking around the yard while our Diggers kept a close watch on things. The warmth of the sun came through, augmenting the heat from the handmade fifty-five-gallon wood burner that sat on some bricks just at the end of the judge's large desk.

A typical wood-burning room heater. This is the PGOV's public shura room where large meetings were held.

The sweets were the homemade kind, similar to rock candy. They lay in a bowl on a small table pushed up against the judge's large desk. In the summer, you would have to wave away a fly or two to get to them. In the deep of winter, that wasn't an issue. However, squeezing my legs between the table and the sofa was. MMJ would often spend the night in his office, sleeping on this sofa.

There were several chairs along the wall on the business side of the desk where the judges sat and two more crammed into the space just inside the door, on the other end of the sofa, for the representatives of each group awaiting their hearing. This at best twelve-foot by ten-foot room was where MMJ held court, slept, and welcomed visitors.

There were several young men always nearby. They were his sons. Of his two oldest, Salam was always smiling, and I would get to know him well. However, MMJ's oldest son, whom I never got to know, had only a month longer to live. He would be killed defending his father in an assassination attempt in late February. It was the event that would triggered the events that led to MK being appointed PCOP.

This day, the elders MMJ had gathered inside the court of appeals building called the elder representative of each of the two groups sitting outside into this small office. They were distinguished from the judges and elders sitting in the room in that neither was wearing white clothing. Their turbans and clothing generally were different shades of brown and gray. The group MMJ had assembled wore white turbans and had white shirts and trousers accompanied by dark vests. All carried a much-needed accessory, a fine wool blanket folded in a manner over one of their shoulders. This was wrapped around the head and body if they became cold, but the fire in the potbelly stove was providing adequate warmth this day. I always wore Carhart long johns and undershirts under my 511 trousers and shirt. The cold would creep in otherwise. The two elders each spoke in turn laying out their case for ownership of the disputed property. Both had deeds and letters showing how the land was titled to each of them. However, they were not from the same government entity but a combination of papers from the last Kingdom, the Communist government, the Soviets, several mujahedeen, the Taliban government, tribal documents, and GIRoA. There were issues concerning access to water involved also. I just thought, *What a mess. How can anyone come to a result that the two groups will accept?* However, I would learn that the subsistence level of life here dictated that controversy needed to end quickly. No one had time to drag things out because that would threaten lives. Being in the fields and working the farms was essential to life here. Winter was unforgiving, and spring was around the corner.

After the two had given their positions in front of each other, the judges asked one to step out, and they began seeking from the other what he and his group really needed out of a compromise. They repeated the same procedure with the other. Afterward, they spent the time talking things through amongst themselves. The compromise resulted in some of the land being split while access to the water was granted to all. MMJ told them he would write out copies for both groups and send another to the judge in Deh Rawud while keeping another copy. They all would sign each copy, thereby making all originals, and one would be kept in the records room of the appeals court. That was it.

MMJ and I then spent some time getting to know each other. I told him how the people in Iraq used the Arab name of Jafer instead of Jeff. We laughed together when I told him I had heard all the Jafer jokes though I confessed I didn't understand most of them. It seems there are many words in Arabic that sound similar to Jafer, and playing on that is an Arab comic's staple. I spoke of the American native tribes and my affiliation with members of such back home. We spoke of the Shawnee, Iroquois, and Miami and how the tribes in Uruzgan shared similar issues today as the American tribes did back in the 1600s and 1700s. I discussed with him Jan's concept of the legal shura, bringing all those entities that have concerns with criminal justice in Uruzgan together to discuss issues facing them. I told him of my difficulties in getting in to see Juma Gul, the PCOP at that time. MMJ said he also had such difficulty but that he would invite him to the next legal shura. That didn't bode well for a functioning criminal justice system in Uruzgan, and it set the tone for the next two years. He went on to give me a complete rundown on the staffing of the courts in Uruzgan, and he complained about how difficult it was to get three judges from the same court to sit on any one case and how funding was in constant short supply. There were two judges who came in from Kabul to hear security cases, but they rarely stayed more than a week. Less than thirty major crimes had cleared the docket in the past year. This resulted in the prison, a home that had been commandeered for the purpose, being extremely overcrowded. This house only had four rooms inside the compound in which to house the prisoners. Their solution was to dig a large hole in the center of the walled house where the garden would have been. They then covered it with logs, rugs and dirt to house the overflow prison population. We agreed we had much to talk about and that we should gather every week, two at the outside, to see what could be accomplished.

Initially our meetings were filled with MMJ speaking to me about the formal structure of the court and its structural shortfalls in Uruzgan. My probes concerning MK's peace shura were met with him decrying its illegitimacy and denials of any involvement with such shuras in the area, for there were several tribal shuras operating too. He spoke of what he thought the ISAF rule of law advisor wanted to hear. It was a beginning that would see great changes while much remained the same in this timeless region disconnected from Kabul.

That which we did accomplish came painfully slow. I continued to connect the dots of Afghan relationships, the money flow, and coordination of the several training efforts to form a goal-oriented ISAF rule of law effort at MNBTK. However, the main undercurrent of how things worked in Uruzgan would flow against what the international community wanted implemented. Developing a new river so the two forces could reach a synergy to bring stability as soon as possible would need MMJ's trust and cooperation. It would also need MMJ to embrace a long-term approach that necessitated working with those who had been brutal against his tribe. This meant working with MK. Watching things unfold after MMJ and I had our morning tea in his office was always a treat. I became, in his eyes, his friend and one he felt comfortable with speaking to in frank terms. We not only talked about our sons but our daughters and wives. That crossing over into conversations concerning the females in our family was evidence of our close relationship, as best it could be under the situation. His parting gift for me in January 2013 was a rather nice intimate evening outfit for my wife. He said to me, "This is a gift for your wife to wear for you." My interpreter pulled me aside and told me that this type of gift was only given to persons who were like brothers to each other, a very close brother. He was wide eyed with how personal of a gift this represented. I must confess that I miss our time together. He is a very wise man, not a saint but wise. My Aussie TF-66 contacts, while working with their Afghan QRF partners, found several kilos of opium in the back of his vehicle one day, which only confirmed my belief that opium was the tie that bound all power in Uruzgan, and it was the key to stability.

Provincial Prosecutor: Anybody Home?

The chief prosecutor's position would be filled over and over again with someone from outside Uruzgan. They would last a few months at best before leaving in disgust while the few local prosecutors would quietly continue on. Reaching that needed accommodation with the realities of Uruzgan would be hard for those sent by the attorney general's office in Kabul, a ministry well known for corruption. I often suspected they came for a cut of the action on the opium trade. Though in fairness I have no direct evidence of that. What I do know is the last two prosecutors, both well educated, came crashing in like bulls in a china shop, aligning themselves with the PGOV who is also an outsider, making public accusations of corruption, which offended the group, while arresting people on the orders of the governor without a warrant, which the judges would overturn. MK would comply with that judicial order, which infuriated the PGOV. Being outsiders, it would take time and a willingness to work into the group, and this behavior hampered that. This constant shifting made it difficult to work effectively with the office directly, so again USAID and EUPOL training was directed at the younger prosecutors while the political squabbling of the chief prosecutor went on. This void crippled the civil prosecutor's office and was a source of instability. If a criminal justice system is crippled, then the populace from which an insurgency gains support suffers and becomes disenfranchised from the government. They don't care if political crimes are prosecuted as much as they do regular criminal acts that involve them. This was a concept that was underserved by the justice sector in Uruzgan, and the justice group needed to coalesce in an effort to address that.

Broken Pieces: Uruzgan Justice Sector in January 2011

Jan, Richelle, and I spent much of our time in January and February 2011 getting all the justice sector actors to come to the monthly legal shura (meeting). Calling, cajoling, and rounding them up became frustrating. Jan's cell phone list was split between us, with each of us calling the people we worked with the most. Richelle brought in Dr. Stanikzai from the Afghan International Human Rights Commission (AIHRC), and the local Ministry of Justice director, Sadat, whilst Jan and I worked on the judges and prosecutors and through them tried to bring in the PCoP. Additionally, Richelle and I were charged with creating a roadmap to guide the PRT rule of law efforts over the next years. The decisions we made over January and February concerning what we believed would work were outside the mold being pushed by the US State Department but was welcomed by the Australian government, which dictated the direction Uruzgan PRT would take. More on that later, but for now it is good to know that the approach was later embraced by the US embassy and allowed us to be out in front of the curve.

In early 2011, the chief civil prosecutor's office, which did not handle Taliban criminals, and the MOJ Department of the Huquq (Rights) were housed in a very dilapidated building where the roof was falling into the chief prosecutor's office, not to mention the auto half-buried at the front area of the house. At that time, the chief prosecutor's position was temporarily being held by a local man, Mirwais Ghani, a stout, rotund man with a big smile and always good for a laugh. He had come down from Chora when the security situation deteriorated and became the prosecutor that handled the cases that went to appeal. He had replaced a man named Abdullah Salihi Khan, who had stepped down to pursue a position in the provincial council. He shared an office with another, a city prosecutor, Mahmud. Mahmud and Salihi were very close, and corruption issues revolved around both of them. Salihi would later return to the prosecutor's office briefly as chief and then move to juvenile prosecutor, while Mahmud would be transferred out due to his corrupt behaviors. There was only one prosecutor outside TK, and that was Shah Mohammad in Deh Rawud. He constantly berated the young DR district judge, Abdul Wahid, because he had no legal training. The civil prosecutor's office would be in turmoil most of time I was there, with infighting and constant replacement of the chief civil prosecutor. From 2010 to March 2014, there would be six chief civil prosecutors: Abdullah Salihi Khan, Mirwais Ghani, Abdullah Salihi Khan (again), Ghulam Farooq Mustafar, Abdul Hadi Hamkar, Ghulam Ghawose Rawoothi, and he resigned in February 2014. That said, in December 2010 this humble shambles of an office was deeply involved in a case that held a high-profile international following. A Taliban judge, a husband and father-in-law, facially mutilated a woman from the area north of the city of Chora by the name of Bibi Aisha. This was done based on claims she had unjustly fled her husband. Unfortunately, this was not an atypical punishment in the region. It is meant as a warning to all women not to leave their husbands. The full story is very revealing about the culture in this rural region of Afghanistan, for she wasn't punished for just leaving her husband. No, it was for doing it in a way that dishonored him and his family.

Bibi Aisha photo by Jodi Bieber / Institute of Time, fall of 2010

The story, related to me by the prosecutor Mahmud and others, involved Aisha fleeing not only an abusive husband but also his family. Aisha had been a child bride, and at age nineteen she had had enough of the abuse and fled her husband's home, returning to her father's home. Her father went to the husband's home and complained about the abuse of his daughter. The families agreed that the abuse would stop, and Aisha's father returned her to her husband's home. There was some confusion as to whether this happened a second time. However, what is certain is that Aisha fled again—this time not to her father's home but to another village. This took the dispute outside of the family, and that dishonored her husband's family. When her husband caught her, the perceived dishonor upon his family was the real offense that warranted the mutilation in the eyes of the Taliban judge.

In addition to her nose being cut off, Aisha's ears were also cropped. She was brought to an NGO near the UPRT Chora detachment and taken to Kabul for treatment. There the special women's crime prosecutor became involved. They took statements from her, and then she was taken to the United States for medical treatment. The area north of Chora is extremely rugged and mountainous. It was at that time a Taliban-controlled area where the police only went into at the risk of losing several officers in the process. Therefore, no efforts we made to apprehend the people involved. A few months later, her father-in-law, a man named Saliman, came into the Tarin Kowt bazaar where he was arrested and placed in the local prison. Shortly thereafter, a request came to the Tarin Kowt prosecutor's office to send Saliman to Kabul for prosecution. That is when Tim and I came into the picture.

Mahmud presenting his case concerning Bibi Aisha

We were on a visit to the prosecutor's office when Mahmud brought the issue to our attention. At that time, there were no public defenders to represent Saliman's interests, so the prosecutor did take the accused's interest into consideration. He also felt a little insulted that Kabul didn't think that his office could handle the case. There may have been some local politics involved, but he genuinely seemed to be handling the situation in a very professional manner. He asked our opinion as to whether he should comply with the request or fight it. Tim and I both asked him what the criminal procedure code dictated. Mahmud told us that under Afghan law the accused was to be tried in the jurisdiction where the crime occurred. We both were aware of the high political profile nature of the situation; however, our mandate was to mentor the justice sector to follow rule of law concepts. So we suggested to Mahmud that he raise the issues presented by the Afghan criminal procedure rules with the Kabul prosecutor's office and see where it went. Weeks later, he proudly reported that he made the argument before the Kabul court, and they had agreed. He showed us copies of the statements taken from Aisha and allowed us to have them read to us by our interpreter. There were some discrepancies in her statement concerning where events happened that only a local would recognize. Mahmud and subsequent prosecutors did reach out to us to establish a videoconference with Aisha in the States. They wished to go over her statements with her to bring clarity to the inconsistencies. Attempts to do that were worked through the US embassy. Understandably, the NGO, who was caring for Aisha in the States, communicated back that it was not possible given her mental state. Even so, Saliman was held without trial for almost a year before he was released on a guarantee, or what we call a bond. He returned to the area north of Chora, and well into 2012, someone at the US embassy would occasionally raise the issue of going in to arrest him again. Matiullah Khan, then the provincial chief of police (PCOP), would say quite fairly, "What thinking drives risking losing several of my ANP for the mere possibility of capturing anyone in that region?" The affair faded into the background noise of the violent nature of the region as Aisha began a new life with a sponsor family in America.

The civil prosecutors in 2010 and until January 2012 were not guarded at all, had no means of transport, and had very bad relations with the provincial police. That made life difficult for them because in the Afghan legal system they held the responsibility for investigating crime. Along with the civil prosecutor is the military prosecutor's office held by Mohammad Zai Khan. Though his office was the internal affairs division of the police, which dealt with crimes committed by police while on duty, his office was also shackled with lack of a security detail, no transportation, and little cooperation, if any, from the then PCOP Juma Gul.

The court where MMJ lived and worked had a leaking roof, as did the primary court building. The state of the infrastructures of the prosecutor and courts reflected the status of their office. They were present in the Uruzgan but not functioning well. Such was the state of dysfunction between the police, prosecutor, and courts at that time. The people of Tarin Kowt didn't know who to go to with their issues, and so they went to the one where they felt most comfortable. That most often was a tribal shura or the Taliban court that roamed the area.

On the other hand, the Afghan National Police (ANP) forces in the province, though well housed and awaiting a new multimillion-dollar complex to be completed at the edge of TK, were in a shambles from a criminal justice system standpoint. From top to bottom, the lack of policing education was appalling. The provincial ANP was nothing but another militia in blue at the beck and call of the provincial chief of police (PCoP). There were only a few professional police in the officer ranks, and the rank and file of the ANP was highly illiterate and trained as, in the terms of the Australian Federal Police mentors, a light infantry unit to essentially augment the Afghan National Army (ANA). The PCoP at that time was a man named Juma Gul. He was highly corrupt, maintaining hundreds of ghost members on his police force and thereby collecting pay for ANP that didn't exist. He was in a constant rivalry with the DR district chief of police (DCoP), Omar Khan, to the point they once engaged in a fistfight at a local shura, narrowly avoiding a gunfight, over allegations of who was the most corrupt. Omar was a shrewd young man who saw an opportunity to advance by helping the US Special Operations Command out of Camp Ripley, and he took it, rising from a cook at an SF FOB in Deh Rawud to the district's chief of police. Omar is a Noorzai, and that was a base for his power in DR, a predominately Noorzai area. He was rumored to have control of the poppy trade in the DR area. Though I never personally confirmed it, I did joke with him about it all the time. He would always tell me he was just a farmer. I would pause and look around the valley at all the purple flowers in bloom on the poppy plants. Then with a large swiping motion of my outstretched hand while my other hand was on his shoulder, I'd say to him, with a smile, "Your crop is doing well, I see." That young brown face highlighted by large white teeth would explode into a huge laugh as he threw his head back while slapping me on the back. Old men were respected in Uruzgan, and frank speech without criticism revealed much.

Much of our frustration with the ANP was that they involved themselves in dispute resolution rather than referring matters to the prosecutor's office or the court. Even more frustrating was the fact that the US Police Mentoring unit was very guarded as to who got to work with the PCoP and DCoPs. I had to find ways around that CTU roadblock during my first year at the PRT. In the background of all of this stood a colonel of ANP, Matiullah Khan, with his own private militia, the KAU.

Unlike the civil prosecutor's offices, the political crimes prosecutor (a.k.a. national defense section prosecutor or NDS) had a nice, well-guarded building. This office was responsible for prosecuting the Taliban, and it spoke volumes about the government priorities concerning establishing a criminal justice system. He was a colonel in the NDS services, had his own vehicle, and enjoyed high status with the provincial police and the Afghan National Army (ANA) commander. Col. Hanif had been in the NDS prosecutor position for several years, and as a result, his office was well organized and very effective compared to the other two prosecutors' office. He was a stern-looking man who had served under the old communist regime. He wasn't much taken to frivolity, and early on, while I was still coming to be able to remember who was who, I mistook him for the former senator from the region. He seemed genuinely upset and scowled at me as we talked. I promised to always remember him in the future, and he and I would play off the incident over time with a big laugh between us. I once introduced him to a colleague of mine from Kandahar Air Field as the man who almost shot me. Hanif just threw his head back in a loud, roaring laugh that seemed to seal our mutual respect for each other. Hanif was very keen on the trainings the PRT was able to bring in. He also understood my desire to have all the prosecutors in the area as well trained as his group, and he participated faithfully in all the legal shuras. He became a man who the people trusted and would seek out to help with all sorts of issues as time went on.

Those who had worked the rule of law piece within the US PRT, that handed over operations to the Dutch a few years before the Australians took over, had worked mainly with the former Taliban government judge, Taj Mohammed. He was moved to head the civil branch of the court of appeals, being replaced by Malavi Mohammad Jan (MMJ) shortly after the Dutch had taken over the PRT efforts. USAID funds had built a courthouse that was being used as the provincial appeals court, manned by basically three judges, all of who held religious titles. Malavi Hammidullah, who was dismissed from his position as appeals judge but brought back by MMJ, sat as the criminal division judge. I would later learn his daughter was MK's fourth wife. Taj Mohammad sat as the civil division judge. (A bomb placed at the local mosque at the time and place he was known to come and pray killed Taj in 2012. The main suspect was his son, who had strong ties to the Taliban.) These three were the backbone of the appeals court, though several other judges, particularly Mohammad Tahib, who heard political/terror crimes, came, sat on some cases, and then left. The primary court in Tarin Kowt, with Judges Haji Abdul Wahid Acheckzai and his son-in-law Abdul Razeeq, operated out of one of five houses built originally by the Dutch to entice judges to come to Tarin Kowt. That didn't happen. Instead the other four houses were leased out to the MOI to house their military prosecutor, Mohammad Zai Khan, and other sections of the provincial police HQ. Both of the primary court judges were educated men, but neither held a law faculty degree. They did, however, attend USAID courses that trained them in the area of the new constitution and its laws. This court was a major source of corruption during my time. Acheckzai had been dismissed as mayor of TK in 2009, and MMJ brought him on as a judge at that time. The only other courts were in the city of Deh Rawud (DR) and Chora. The court in DR was manned by Abdul Wahid, who had been the tutor of the children of the previous PGOV, Jan Mohammad Khan. Abdul Wahid would prove to be ineffective and a source of much consternation for the district during my years in Uruzgan. A very old mullah, by the name of Mohammad Doad, manned the court in Chora. He was symbolic at best and in poor health. There was also a mullah, Eid Mohammad, in Gizab appointed by MMJ as a judge but never confirmed by the HJC. Since Gizab was constantly being placed in and out of Day Kundi province, he never came into the conversations much at all.

Tarin Kowt held the provincial prison operated under the Ministry of Justice (MOJ). The government of the Netherlands was building a nice, modern, concrete prison not far from the new police headquarters being built by the US Army Corps of Engineers. The prison opened late in 2011, and the new police facility, which was a huge, walled compound with multiple guard towers and included several military-style barracks inside, wouldn't be open until late 2012. In the meantime, the prisoners were held in a mud-walled compound that sat on about a three-quarter-acre lot, with it being about a one hundred feet wide where the entrance was located on a main street in Tarin Kowt. The gray mud walls rose about forty feet along the edges of the lot. If one would look down upon the lot from the street side, you would see a rectangle-shaped, walled lot with one large structure in the left corner and another smaller, narrow building running along the back wall. A twenty-five-foot interior wall with a barred iron gate big enough for one person to go through ran from the back right corner of the large structure to the wall. A smaller structure, which housed the guards, sat just to the right of the gate before one entered the prison yard. There were mud steps carved into the side of the large structure that allowed one to climb upon the roof and look down into the prison yard. So entry into the prison required one to enter the main gate and step into a small courtyard, then wait until that gate was secured before proceeding into the main yard through the smaller locked gate in the interior wall. There were two rooms in the large structure that housed the prisoners. The smaller structure along the back wall contained three toilets. There was a pond in the main courtyard where the prisoners bathed and often took water for cooking. Looking down from the roof of the large structure, you could the large hole in the center of the courtyard that was the entrance to the underground room that had been created to handle the over 120 male prisoners held there.

Conditions, shall we say, were rough. However, the prisoners were resilient. They prepared and cooked their own meals, which meant they had access to small knives and small propane gas containers. When Jan first took me there, he and I conversed with the prisoners, and most, not all, were congenial. There were a few who were obviously Talib who kept their distance and threw their contempt at us by the look in their eyes and the scowls on their faces. However, we were seeking to find those held beyond their sentencing dates and to help with humanitarian needs, such as blankets and bedding. That effort was warmly received. The Afghans in Uruzgan have a different sense of being a prisoner. Jan reported to me that once the west wall of the prison collapsed, but nobody attempted to escape. Also, there were incidents of tribal elders sending someone to the prison for an offense they deemed required them to spend time in the prison. The person would just show up and declare that the tribal elders sent him to be imprisoned. When asked for how long, they would respond, "Until they say I can return to the village." The prisoner director would let them in and place them in with the inmates until such time as the elders came to bring him home.

The Slovakian and Dutch governments provided sorely needed blankets and other humanitarian needs to the prison at this time. To assist in housing within this small space, they delivered two large field tents. They erected one, and the other just went missing, never to be seen again.

The Legal Shura: Jan Plants the Seed of His Legacy

Jan Wilken had worked months to get the personnel from the Uruzgan legal sector to meet on a regular basis to discuss common problems. He set the first legal shura for early January 2011 and was finally able to bring them together on January 8 at the PGOV's compound. The day came, and we rolled out at 0800 to be there by 0830. We pulled up to the main gate and rolled right in. This was a luxury that would change by mid-2011. We approached the guards at the gate that led into the PGOV's main area that contained the building where the meeting was set for. The guard knew nothing of the meeting but allowed us to enter the area. Jan immediately grabbed Sadat, the EUPOL interpreter, and they were on the phone. I would learn that due to the colder weather, Uruzganis don't get an early start in the winter. The weather dictated everything. In the heat of summer, we would get our meetings going by 0800 to avoid the heat. In the winter, we would wait until 0900 to allow for the sun to warm the rooms, and even then it was a slow start.

Over the next hour, representatives from the all the separate prosecutor offices, MOJ, AIHRC, the prison director, and judges, including MMJ, arrived. I met both the NDS prosecutor Col. Hanif and the Uruzgan senator to the Afghan parliament, Senator Hanifi, at this time. I was still trying to distinguish one turbaned and bearded person from the next and the fact that they both dressed in similar garb made the distinction even harder. That would cause a few moments of discomfort between Col. Hanif and me down the road when I publicly mistook him for Senator Hanifi. With each wave of individuals, there was much hugging and bearded kisses to the cheeks. This ritual would repeat itself each time such a gathering occurred. Manners matter in Afghanistan.

Legal shura at PGOV's compound hosted by MMJ. The un-turbaned man on the left is the ILF-A public defender.

The shura was opened by MMJ, with him asking Haji Abdul Wahid to lead the group in prayer. That would repeat itself at the end of the meeting, not dissimilar to local governmental gatherings in the United States. This was how it would always be with this group. The main highlight at this gathering was the fact that the Deh Rawud district judge, Abdul Wahid, the former tutor for Jan Mohammad Khan's (JMK) children, had come to address the group, and Jan had brought his *fotbul* (soccer for the English speaking) league's official scarves as gifts to all he was saying good-bye to. Abdul Wahid laid out a very disturbing picture in Deh Rawud. The district chief of police and local drug lord Omar Khan continued to threaten the judge's life if he interfered with how the DCoP ran the area. Now it wasn't the whole story, and over the next years I became privy to how incompetent and corrupt the judge was. He was so bad that MMJ had to bring him to Tarin Kowt for protection when he, for some reason, took bribes from one party to convict someone and then took bribes from the other party to release that person. This judge had a long way to go but, he could read and write, so for now he was the judge of Deh Rawud. It was part of the fabric of the region that struggles under the weight of high illiteracy rates. Jan's scarf party was a big success though. Not only were the scarves colorful and unique but very useful in the cold of winter. I gathered them all for a group photograph, and amid the jovial teasing and laughter, hope was shining as bright as the day's winter sun.

The first legal shuras would sputter, stall, and restart, but with no PCoP in attendance, they always fell short of expectations, because without the security of the police, nonpolitical crimes investigations were near to impossible. More importantly, it was clear by the conversations between those that did attend that the police themselves, they being more of a militia, were a source of instability because of their behavior. At best, they were taking fees for passage through checkpoints and at worst were beating and abusing the population, running them down with their vehicles and abusing the young boys of the area. The PCoP, Juma Gul, was an overweight despot who cared only for his own position shown by his corrupt behavior of taking money meant to staff his force, thus underserving the area. However, worse than that, he had no passion for his job, which I'm sure he received through patronage, and Taliban police and courts flourished in the outlying areas away from Tarin Kowt, Deh Rawud, and Chora. He was a prime example of MMJ's statement that outsiders come to use Uruzgan to line their pockets.

A Stroll in the Park: A Vice Admiral Drags the Minister of Justice Down to Uruzgan

Mid-January 2011 saw Jan's time winding down rapidly, and the week following the legal shura a US State Department legal education program called the Justice Sector Support Program (JSSP) had been scheduled. Ted had used that program as the reason why I needed to come straight to Tarin Kowt from Kabul, bypassing Kandahar Air Field (KAF). However, it was cancelled three days beforehand, but "no worries," as the Aussie's would say, there was always something filling in the time. On this occasion, it happened to be the arrival of the Afghan minister of justice. Now, no minister of any chamber of the government in Kabul had ever come to Uruzgan, so this was a big deal. However, as with most all such events, it was happening because a high-ranking ISAF officer was making it happen. In this case, it was Vice Admiral Robert S. Harward who was heading up Combined Joint Interagency Task Force 435, which was charged, among many other things, to bring the detention systems out of the Stone Age. The Dutch prison project was almost complete, and by God that minister of justice was going to come down to Uruzgan and view the prison situation. The vice admiral was a commander of Navy SEALs, and he brought down with him his command master chief (CMC), a man by the name of Edwards, for whom I swore the term "tough as nails" was coined. The two of them were a force unto themselves that could be felt from one hundred meters away. The minister of justice had been reluctant to come to Uruzgan because he feared for his life. However, he was no match for the admiral, and he was coming to Uruzgan.

These VIP arrivals are rarely longer than the day, more like hours, to get the VIPs back to the safety or "higher" meetings in Kabul or Kandahar. This was no exception, and it was a whirlwind. The admiral's plane, with the minister strapped in, arrived early in the morning. The PRT and CTU commands arranged vehicles to bring them up from the flight line for a quick meeting and briefing of what was to follow. The minister was met by the flight line by the PGOV and his security force. They took him directly to the PGOV's compound for some private time before the admiral's entourage with Jan and me in tow would arrive. I always found the lack of the higher military officer's interest in what Jan and I had to say absolutely amazing. The focus was on the CTU command, which was at this moment represented by Australian Col. Malone. Col. Malone was a tall, commanding man with good humor. He had already pulled Jan and me into his office the evening before for a complete briefing on our activities concerning the prison. The meeting started with that great Australian fresh openness about the reality of the situation, which he stated using the great Australian adjective "fuck" and its derivatives that are used to describe most such situations. It went something along the lines of the visit had been announced quickly and without much notice because the minister was afraid of being (Aussie adjective inserted here) attacked in Uruzgan. After getting his frustration out, he just said with a smile, "Where does the situation concerning the prison (insert Aussie adjective here) stand?" The man was delightfully refreshing, and we were glad to let him be the focus. However, he did state as we left his office that evening, "You're both coming along, right?" or some such thing. Jan smiled and said, "Of course, you'll need us to find the place." We just laughed.

The next morning, Jan and I met for an early breakfast and the mandatory relaxed cup of cappuccino from the coffee machine. We liked to sit out in the warming sun on the cold Uruzgan winter mornings if the sun so graced us with its presence. It did this morning, so we pulled some chairs from the Windmill's deck and brought them to a spot where the rays of the sun were just coming over the mountain ridge.

The Windmill

Jan was going home soon, and I could tell he didn't want to. He had managed two six-month extensions from both his government and EUPOL, but now it was over. He just sat there and told me all he could about the relationships, what he had done and what he felt needed to be accomplished. I listened throughout the time it took to enjoy our cappuccinos without rushing. Time was slowing down for me, moving more toward Afghan time. With a pause at the end of his comments and while looking over toward the mountains, Jan and I sat in silence. Then I said to him, "Jan, the key is in getting the legal shura to the point where they own it. It is the one group that can bring stability because it is based on their cultural ideal of elders meeting to reach consensus. It differs only in that it is made up of elders who hold government positions." He nodded his agreement, and then as we stood up and began moving our chairs back, he said, "The involvement of the police in that shura is critical." I responded with a glib, "Yeah, you got that right." He just laughed, and off we went to get our gear, stopping at the latrine along the way as the coffee took hold, a necessity that had to be answered before venturing outside of MNBTK, for the toilet facilities in Tarin Kowt were not a pleasant experience.

I once took the time on several occasions to count the number of strides from my chalet 17 to the PRT chalet E, and it was about six hundred to seven hundred strides between them, depending on how quickly I was moving and the length of the stride that generated. It was about five hundred yards or so. Enough to keep the weight down, I would learn later when I moved over to Camp Ripley and had access to a Toyota pickup truck all the time. Jan and I met at the center of the Camp Holland outside the DEFAC at the volleyball courts. In just a few months, a great tournament would be played between all the units, including Afghan military and all the interpreter's teams. The temperature that July day would climb near to 40 degrees Celsius, but today I had my long johns on under my 511 trousers and shirt, which ensured my comfort while in Tarin Kowt. The Bushies rolled up, and soon the admiral and his staff arrived. Jan and I were placed in the same Bushie as the CMC, and we had a chance to enjoy his perspective of the situation in Afghanistan as we rolled along. Jan shared his stories concerning the prison and the episode of the wall falling down while all the prisoners remained within the compound.   Reaching   the compound, we rolled to our usual site and dismounted. It appeared we were going to walk the distance from the PGOV's compound to the prison. It wasn't all that far, a little more than a quarter of a mile. However, today the admiral set the agenda, and he wasn't wearing his body armor for the walk. He stated quit firmly he wanted to send the message that the streets were safe. He didn't want to be seen taking less of a risk than the minister was taking.

It wasn't like we weren't well guarded. I for one was glad to drop the gear. At age sixty, the body armor took its toll on me over the long haul. However, I could hear the scolding from Diplomatic Security should they get wind of what happened that day. The hammer would fall soon enough after an over energetic non-career State Department PRT person down in Helmand brought along a journalist to document his activities off the reservation. He was fluent in Pashtu and would often drive off alone without a personal security detail to visit elders or ride along with the local Afghan Police commander. It was touted as the way it should be done by the journalist, as if this particular person was the only one doing it. We were all taking risks to be as personal and integrated with our Afghan counterparts as we could. When the article hit the national press, all the boundaries that many hardworking and dedicated US State Department PRT members were pushing to get maximum impact in their areas were shut down. All I can say to this selfish, ego-driven person is thanks for screwing it all up for the rest of us. Suddenly there could be no more trips to Chora or Khas Uruzgan to meet elders because the base there was deemed too insecure for overnight visits. It was a huge blow to my efforts in linking those areas back to the justice sector in Tarin Kowt.

The entourage with the admiral at the lead, Col. Malone at his side, followed by the rest, walked out the front gate of the PGOV's compound and took a right, heading toward the prison. The walk was very interesting, with all the locals looking on. The minister, however, was nowhere in sight. He, it seemed, had decided to be driven by the PGOV's bodyguards. The locals seemed stunned, and my thought at the time was that we took them by surprise with such a large crowd and the only ones wearing body armor were the troops providing protection. Surprise, a typical SEAL tactic served us well that day.

A walk in the park to the old prison with the vice admiral

We arrived well ahead of the minister, and the guards were all gathered in as fine of a military formation as they could muster. It was a bit humorous, but they were giving it their all. The problem was they didn't know the admiral and couldn't understand why such a large group of foreigners had shown up on a day they were expecting the most senior official of the ministry where they were employed. There was no way they were going to allow anyone through those gates until their minister arrived. There began a confused conversation between the interpreter of the admiral, who was from Kabul and therefore a Dari speaker, and the commander of the prison, Bishmullah, a Pashtu speaker. Throw in the Uruzgan dialect, and things were going downhill fast. I found Jan and his interpreter, Saba, who were hanging outside by the road, talking to prison guards they knew. I grabbed them both, saying as we went, "They don't know the admiral, and they could care less who he is. You need to get in there and sort this out." When Jan broke through the crowd, Bishmullah smiled and raised his hand in greeting to Jan. I watched as the effect of time spent with these people showed its power. Hugs and relieved cheerful conversation flowed. Jan and Saba had it all sorted out in a few moments. He turned to the admiral and explained Bishmullah had been given orders to wait for the minister. To his credit, the admiral went with the flow, not pushing the issue, and engaged Bishmullah in conversation about how the prison was operating and what shortfalls he was experiencing while they waited for the minister to arrive.

The minister's motorcade arrived, and I watched as this elderly man dressed in fine white and yellow clothing, topped by a white turban and highlighted by his white beard, hesitantly made his way across the muddy street and into the squalor of the prison compound. Bishmullah and his guards snapped to attention, and all executed their best salutes possible. It reminded me of an old comedy on US television back in the 1960s called *F-Troop*, about a troop of cavalry soldiers on the American western frontier whose members were just a half beat off on their execution of their military duties. However, it was a noble effort by all, and they were proud of themselves.

Entering the prison compound, Jan and I took the lead in explaining to the admiral and the CMC how the place was operated with the inmates preparing their own food, therefore having access to knives to peel the potatoes and cannabis plants being grown in the main yard.

The prisoners gathered around the minister of justice, who was standing on the edge of the water supply inside the prison scene in the foreground

A few months later, it would be a different story when a US Army brigadier general brought the head of prisons from the Ministry of Interior from Kandahar when that ministry took control of them. Instead of a confident, relaxed, and engaged admiral, I had to contend with an uptight army general who scolded Bishmullah for allowing the prisoners to have knives to prepare their food. The general actually asked why they didn't have an outside service provider serving the food. That question was so obtuse to the reality of Uruzgan I could only stare at him in disbelief.

CMC checking out the "flower" garden in the old prison

However, on this day, the admiral and CMC didn't hesitate to go into the underground quarters or speak directly with the inmate peeling his potatoes. However, the minister did not feel as comfortable, nor did he take advantage of the underground part of the tour.

The vice admiral disappears into the underground cell

The minister gave a grand speech and then departed in a swirl of dirt as his motorcade sped back to the safety of the PGOV's compound. The admiral said his good-byes, and we started the trek back also. On the way back, he asked if any minister from the Kabul government had ever come to Uruzgan without accompanying an ISAF general officer. Jan told him this was the first minister, to his knowledge, that ever made the trip to Uruzgan. We wouldn't see another until late in the summer of 2012. The good news would be that several would come, and they would not be in the company of any ISAF general officers.

Returning to the PGOV's compound, we sat in on a news conference with the Afghan press and television interviewing the minister of justice. Thereafter, a large lunch was served where Haji Abdul Wahid, Judge Hamidullah, Jan, and I shared the main course platter. Jan and I were impressive with our use of the flatbread for consuming the delicacy of fatty lamb.

The author and Haji Abdul Wahid

Jan and Hamidullah with Aussie legal officer Major O'Shea

MOJ press conference

Roadmap: Figure out What the Community Is Naturally Doing to Administer Justice and Mentor from There

Between VIP visits and meetings with MMJ in January and early February 2011, I read every article of Thomas Barfield's that I could get my hands on. I read every report concerning Hamid Karzai's rise to power, starting with his activities in Uruzgan with the American Special Forces. I sat with the Australian Department of Foreign Affairs and Trade (DFAT) Uruzgan tribal guru Joel McGregor, who was pleased to inform me that the Crowther name was a sub clan of the McGregor clan, and picked his brain concerning the tribal rivalries that pushed the politics of the Uruzgan. In the meantime, Richelle poured over the several TLO and other NGO reports concerning how the local population viewed justice administration in Uruzgan. We came to the conclusion that the rule of law approach was swimming against the current. One glaring revelation came when I tasked the USAID representative to provide me with a list of the names of the tribal elders from Uruzgan that attended a seminar aimed at what was called the informal rule of law sector. This training was geared toward educating elders on dispute-resolution techniques as well as the constitution of Afghanistan, the rights of women under the law, and other subjects that they hoped would elevate the tribal elders' knowledge to the point where their shura rulings would be seen as more just than the Taliban circuit judges'. I met with resistance in getting the names, and I had to reach high into the Regional Command South USAID representative to force the release of the names. It was a prime example of working against our own interest. What was revealed was most, if not all, of the attendees were members of MK's *ishula* (peace) shura. MK was in the process of creating a shadow government of his own, and this set off warning lights for Richelle and me. That said, we agreed that we would not swim against the current but would embrace it and steer the flow toward incorporating the informal tribal shuras, as much as possible, with the formal justice system, especially the courts. We felt if we could create an interaction between the formal and informal, it could lead to the incorporation of a review process that could put all legal matters under judicial review, and from there they could start moving down the road of using the formal system, with its human rights protections, as the forum of first choice in the future. However, the future was a long way off, and neither of us had the confidence or trust of the Afghans to the point they were freely letting us know what was really happening at all levels of the justice sector in Uruzgan. There were going to be some interesting surprises that would pop out as time went on.

There were two major concerns we both wanted to address. The first was to bring the USAID training to Uruzgan so we would have open access to what training was taking place and with whom. We wanted the training to be diversified across tribal divides so we were seen as working for Uruzgan and not the Popalzai tribe, of which MK was a leading member. The second was getting close cooperation across the justice sector, and that was going to be a tough nut to crack with the present PCOP. I would reach out through my channels to bring the USAID informal justice training to Uruzgan to no avail. Uruzgan, the birthplace of the mullah Omar, who started the Taliban movement, wasn't a "key terrain district" and therefore not a candidate for expenditures of the limited USAID funds. Richelle would work very hard to bring the funding in from the Australian government, and this program would eventually launch in Uruzgan, and in doing so, it would open the doors for a greater cooperation across the province between the tribal elders and the formal justice sector. However, at first MMJ would give mixed signals of how he viewed such cooperation. I didn't want to bring something into the region he would oppose, as I wanted whatever we did to enhance what the Afghans were willing to use. Richelle and I were convinced that we could mentor toward a more modern criminal justice system if we were willing to accept where they were and not attempt to force them down a path they weren't already on. They are years away from such a system, but the foundation of what created modern criminal justice systems was alive and well in Uruzgan. What is a three-judge panel or jury in the Western world other than the modernized tribal elders' council? The biggest impediment to a modern criminal justice system was the militarized police. Traditionally, just like we did back before Sir Robert Peel formed the London Metropolitan Police Force, the Afghans would select several men of the village to go after a wrongdoer. They would then return that person to the village elders for a trial. Once the trial was over, they were released from duty. They worked for the community. However, the Afghan National Police had no sense of serving the community. They were trained as soldiers and served as such. Until we had a PCOP who understood the idea of community-oriented police and a systematic approach to criminal justice, in a formal sense, rule of law was doomed in Uruzgan. We had heard that a professional PCOP was going to replace Juma Gul. We erroneously thought that it would start a new era, but frustratingly, it didn't address the problem.

Colonel Shirazad would up came up from Kandahar in mid-July with much fanfare from the PGOV. He looked every inch a professional, and on paper he was well qualified, but he wasn't from Uruzgan, and the tribal politics and mistrust of outsiders was almost immediate. We were fortunate in that at the time of his arrival a new police mentor, Lieutenant Colonel (LTC) Hefner, was assigned. "Hef" was a likeable guy with a great sense of humor. He wasn't under any illusions about what he could accomplish, but he was very willing to bring the EUPOL advisors and me into his conversations with the PCOP. That helped us because we were no longer blind to what was happening with the PCOP. However, even with this professional PCOP, real community-based policing wasn't a high priority.

During my meetings with MMJ, I was constantly feeling him out for his acceptance of the ideas Richelle and I had projected upon the roadmap. He seemed to give me what I felt was a standard line he thought I wanted to hear, that tribal shuras are bad and government courts were good. I asked him if he was involved at all with the ishula shura held each week at MK's KAU compound. He flatly denied it, and the times I attended, he wasn't there. However, members of the shura told us that "local judges" did review the findings of the shura for proper rulings, especially for women. This cat and mouse game continued for some time between us. It was difficult to get a read on how MMJ really thought about the mix between the court and the traditional justice mechanisms in Uruzgan. I sought to assure him that the training of tribal shura members was not meant to go around his authority as the chief judge of the province but to help educate the tribal leaders on the laws of Afghanistan and that those laws were based in Hanifi sharia. In fact, the NGO that would administer the training would be seeking him out as an advisor to the program as well as a participant. When I told him that many members of MK's ishula shura had been trained already down in Kandahar, he seemed a little concerned. I told him I wanted the trainers for the project here in Uruzgan to seek him out so a balanced approach, involving actual tribal elders from all the tribes, would be the hallmark of the effort. He seemed pleased and satisfied with that explanation and gave his blessing on the project.

I met with MMJ twice in the first three weeks of February, and I noticed that MMJ slept in his office most evenings. He rarely traveled to his home because there had already been two attempts on his life before I arrived. The PCOP at the time, Juma Gul, claimed he didn't have the manpower to protect the courts, even though he was collecting pay for over one thousand ghost police soldiers on his payroll. It was further proof of PCOP Juma Gul's incompetence and greed interfering with progress. I was unsuccessfully trying to get the date for the next legal shura locked in before I left for Kandahar Air Field on February 21 for a conference with other rule of law advisors in RC-S. It would be at that conference where I came to realize the frustration others were having in the lack of progress from the government in Kabul when it came to establishing a criminal justice system in the rural areas in the south of Afghanistan. Arriving back from KAF on the twenty-fourth, I received the news that another assassination attempt had been made against MMJ. He made a rare trip back to his house. They were watching and waiting just down the road. MMJ's car had stopped right outside his home, waiting for the large metal gate, found on the homes of wealthier individuals, to be opened. Two men on a motorcycle raced forward, with the man on the back firing his AK-47. MMJ's son stood his ground, advancing on the attackers and firing as he went. He was fatally struck with several bullets but managed to wound the attackers and saved his father's life. MMJ suffered a severe, glancing head wound. It would be nine days before I would see him. When I did set our next time together, I struggled with a simple question. What do you say to a man who watched his son sacrifice his life to save him? What I really wanted to know was how this event would change him and what it meant for our relationship.

A Long, Quiet Meeting

I found myself walking in the dark, early morning hours of March 5 over the small golf-ball- sized stones that covered the ground to the DFAC coffee shop. My meeting with MMJ was still five hours away. I was struggling with the ideas coming into my head and the depth of the emotions they brought. I found myself stopping at the small makeshift memorial of a single artificial flower stuck in the wire of the HESCO next to the latrine unit where the Dutch female soldiers had been killed. Another male Dutch soldier died that day as he ran alongside the chalet next to the latrine. The puncture holes in the HESCO showed a pattern right at head level, and that is where the flower was stuck. Tim had stopped me one day shortly after arriving, telling me the story as if he didn't want the memory of that event to pass into the oblivion of the endless rotation of personnel. The theater of the mind was in overload; I relived seeing my own father in his death throws, my forced separation from my children that pushed me to the brink of suicide, all the comrades in arms from Vietnam who didn't come home, and the deaths of those I worked with in Iraq, both military and civilian, who had perished pursuing peace or some elusive idea of what that meant. How would the words of an outsider, an invader and infidel, be taken? MMJ and I had spoken of my "book," the Bible, and its Christian messages, and he was receptive to those discussions, but this was unchartered territory for both of us.

Since it was winter, the mission was set to depart at 0930 hours. I had Sahli as my interpreter, which was fortunate, for he and I had discussed the Christian and Muslim faiths at great length, and getting my words correct was critical. Also Sahli had shared his own life's tragedies with me, and that gave me insight not only into how he thought but how Afghans approached life. His own cousin, in an honor killing, murdered Sahli's father. His father, at age fifteen, had been accused of providing the knife that killed his brother-in-law. Though denying the accusations forty years later, his nephew came to him one Friday asking to go to the mosque with him that day. While walking to the mosque, the nephew pulled a gun and shot his uncle, Sahli's father, to death. The police never charged Sahli's cousin, his father's own nephew, with the crime. Sahli said they were bought off and that honor killings rarely are prosecuted. Sahli struggled with what to do. Honor demanded his cousin's death, but at what price to Sahli? There is an old Pashtu saying that a family waited one hundred years to avenge the death of a family member, but the family was scolded by the tribal elders for acting too hastily. I spoke to him of how a killing inflicts damage to the one who does the killing, that he must carry it all his life. Only a hundred years will tell if he took it to heart.

Before leaving, I was able to bounce a few ideas off of Sahli as well as pull up from my mind some conversations with my Iraqi interpreter, Saad. The core value of a son was what I needed to impart, and I didn't know his son or him well enough to be confident of what could or should be said on this day. I settled my head against the back of the rigid plastic chair inside the Bushie and strapped myself in. I closed my eyes and just let the rolling, rugged ride settle in as I let my mind wander, seeking a voice from the universe for guidance.

The man I saw that day was weighed down with grief. He was lying on the sofa in his office when I arrived. He had just arisen from that position as I rounded the corner from the main entrance of this single-level building into his office. Dropping my body armor on the floor, I could see the long wound from the bullet that had grazed his skull was still fresh, and his body appeared weak. We said nothing as our eyes meant. I stood for just a brief moment and then went over and hugged him, kissing his cheeks in the customary Afghan way, and then just held him for a moment. We stepped back from each other and for a moment held onto each other's arms in a friendly embrace. I could not hide my tears, nor would I be able to disguise the emotion in my voice when we did speak. His eyes were sad, and he just looked at me. He broke the silence between us with "Salam Allakum," and I replied in a choked-up voice, "Allakum a Salam." The traditional Islamic greeting of "The peace of God be with you," responded to with "God's peace be upon you." He wrapped himself in a traditional fine wool blanket and proceeded to go around his desk to take his seat while Sahli and I sat down on the recently vacated sofa. The room always smelled of him, that grandfather smell of age.

Soon the tea arrived, as did his son Salam and the criminal division appeals judge, Hamidullah. We all waited in silence as the tea was served. Taj Mohamad, the civil division judge, stepped in, and then MMJ casually broke the silence by saying, "General Petraeus called me to give his condolences." I don't know if the general knew of MMJ before this incident because the incident was well reported throughout the ISAF intelligence network, but it spoke volumes of how well Petraeus understood Afghan culture. That call made a significant impact on MMJ, and it made my job easier that morning.

I said to Mohammad Jan that both my father and uncle had died at the relatively young ages of thirty-eight and thirty-six. "My grandmother, their mother, who was widowed when they were both just young boys, told me of her pain in having to bury her own children. It seems out of the natural order of things, though as older men, we all know that isn't true. God takes us when he wants us," I said. That statement prompted a similar discussion around the room between Taj, MMJ, and Hamidullah. MMJ's speech was steady and growing stronger as we just generally discussed life and its twists. We all agreed that we are fortunate to have God's gift of life each and every day that we have had so far. He spoke of how the incident unfolded until he could speak no more. I then said to MMJ something that I was surprised came out of me. It just came to me as something from my heart. I said, "Malavi Saab, in all this sadness, you have been given a gift from God. You, unlike many men, will always know how much your son loved you. You know how well you raised him and the honor he brought to your family. You will always look up into heaven and walk proudly among the Pashtu as you continue the work God has given you here because of your son's love for you. In all the sadness of these days, I believe that is a tremendous gift." I saw him visibly rise taller in his chair while tears came to his eyes, not a flood but a mist covering his eyes. I changed the subject by asking if additional guards had been sent to protect him.

Hamidullah answered, saying, "Only a few more here but none at his house."

I said to the judges as a whole, "Now is not the time to speak further concerning this. However, we shall meet in a few days, and I will want to know how they think we should move forward. What extra security efforts are needed, and how do we put them in place?"

Upon leaving, all the judges, in typical Afghan custom, walked me to the entrance area. After gearing up, Salam, MMJ's son, approached me with a hug and a sad smile. Turning to MMJ, we hugged, and then holding both his hands together with mine, we just looked into each other's eyes, knowing we didn't have to say anything. He knew I cared for his safety and that I was just as determined as he was to make Uruzgan, and thereby him, safer. I also knew that safety must come from their efforts, not ours. I had slipped into Afghan mode, though I didn't know it at the time.

It would be over a week before I could get back to see MMJ. However, when we again met, he seemed in good spirits. Not only in good spirits but very fired up over the terrorists coming out of Pakistan and how the nations of the world needed to unite against them. He had a guest staying with him from the Knowledgeable Union of Tribal Elders, which is the translation given to me for the Ulema Council, a religious organization that advises parliament on whether the laws passed are proper under Islam. These councils advise all Islamic governments, such as Saudi Arabia, Iran, U.A.E., and Afghanistan.

Our conversation wandered a bit. I could tell he was reevaluating many things. His security situation hadn't changed much, and I begged the obvious unanswered question as to whether he had contacted MK for additional protection. He said that wouldn't be appropriate, given he wasn't the PCOP. I replied, "MK may not be the PCoP, but he is the one who stands to lose the most if you are killed, and he is the one who can protect you the best." I told him to think about it, and though we had a legal shura scheduled for the next week, this discussion should not be public. I would meet privately with him in about a month. In the meantime, I had to travel to Deh Rawud and was also taking time to return to the United States for a few weeks to be with my family. MMJ was traveling to Kabul after the legal shura and would be gone for several weeks also.

Jan's Legacy Blossoms

Jan had left in February, so a few days after my meeting with MMJ, my first legal shura came together. True to form, Richelle and I would again pick up where Jan left off, making cell phone calls to be sure everyone would attend. It wasn't their justice shura yet, and I made a mental note to confront MMJ at the appropriate time as to whether he would take ownership of this forum. The idea hadn't formulated in my mind at the time, but I would start to see the justice sector group as a governance organization that had the possibility to make a significant impact on stability in the area because their decisions impacted the daily lives of the local populations.

As usual, no representative from the provincial Afghan National Police attended. It was held at the appeals court where MMJ was staying. Across the hall from MMJ's office was a large room that had been intended to be the courtroom. It had two large tables and a British-style dock where the prisoner was to sit. I'm not sure they ever used it for a courtroom. I never saw it used so. However, it was perfect for larger gatherings such as this justice sector shura. MMJ wasn't there, but the usual justice sector participants gathered: the primary court judges, Chief Judge Haji Abdul Wahid and his son-in-law Judge Abdul Raziq; the appeals court judges, Hamidullah, Taj Mohammad; the NDS prosecutor, Col. Hanif; the civil prosecutors, Salihi and Mirwais Ghani; the military prosecutor, Mohammad Zai; the prison director, Bishmullah; district judges from Chora and Deh Rawud, old Doad Mohammad and Abdul Wahid respectively; the Huquq director, Abdul Mohammad, and the assistant MOJ director, Abdul Baqi. The two outside the official governmental justice actors were Dr. Stanikzai from the Afghan International Human Rights Commission (AIHRC) and the medical doctor from Tarin Kowt Hospital.

The Huquq Department fell under the Ministry of Justice. The MOJ was, at this time, in charge of the prison, juvenile detention, and public education of Huquq or what we call citizen rights. The Huquq Department also arbitrated civil disputes, and as such the director stood to gain from a bribe or two. The director of the provincial MOJ was Sayeed Mohammad Sadat, whom I had heard about but had never seen because he was in Kabul beating on doors to get the money to operate the local office of the MOJ.

Legal shura at the provincial appeals courtroom with docks
on either side. Left to right: Acheckzai, Col. Hanif and
Dr. Stanikzai, AIHRC director at head of table.

Abdul Baqi was a local man and quietly got things done. It would
be another two months before we would meet Sadat. Sadat was touted
as the best-educated person in the province on civil legal matters.
PGOV Omar Sharizad would call him "the man that knows the law."
It was a blessing and a curse because, being focused on what should
happen legally, he lost the ability to get things accomplished in this
backwater region that operated on relationships. That said, he did push
the others to change their behavior to more closely conform to the law.
His frustration with the local power networks eventually would lead
to his resignation the following year. His Huquq director was always a
thorn in his side. Abdul Mohammad refused to bring his department
physically into a newer compound Sadat would procure for the MOJ
offices. Abdul Mohammad would reveal himself to be quite the jokester
whose cell phone ring tone was a bird song that I would whistle back to
him when we met in public, giving rise to much laughing and manly
backslapping. He was always smiling—all the way to the bank, I'm sure.
He was the brother of both the criminal appeals judge Hamidullah,
whose daughter was married to MK, and the then prison director,

Jeffrey Crowther

Bishmullah. Learning these ties paid off down the road because the patronage networks wielded the power.

Dr. Stanikzai had been in the province for about a year and worked closely with the United Nations Assistance Mission Afghanistan (UNAMA) in monitoring human rights abuses, which were many. He would become a driving force in making this legal shura a major force in the province once I convinced him that reporting human rights abuses was not enough. Solving the problem of such abuses required a functioning criminal justice mechanism in Uruzgan.

After the opening prayer by Haj Abdul Wahid, who was chairing the event, the shura's main discussion revolved around how a prisoner's age could be determined. In Afghanistan, people often only know what season of the year they were born and a loose year. In particular, there was one person who claimed he was seventeen at the time of his arrest and had been held now for over two years. Col. Hanif offered the solution of trying him as an adult, convicting him, and then giving him a two-year sentence with credit for the time he had already been in. It was humorous in this case, but more often the matter was more serious than that. The families would be involved, with the accused's family claiming he was under the age of eighteen and must be treated under the law for juveniles, while the victim's family would insist he was an adult and must be accountable as such. Resolving this in a transparent and scientific way was crucial in these situations, for if the judge or prosecutor was seen as bending to the will of one family or the other, then their lives would be in danger, as such disrespect shown to either family was an insult to that families' honor, and retribution would be demanded under Pashtunwali.

There was one very overworked doctor at the hospital in Tarin Kowt. A simple X-ray of the long bones of the arm would reveal the approximate age of the accused by whether the growth plate had reached maturity and sealed itself. This was considered under the law as the manner in which such issues were resolved. The problem was one family, or the other, was always threatening the doctor's life, especially in political insurgent crimes, which meant the Taliban would make good on the threats. The poor doctor sat at the shura nearly in tears explaining his situation. He was willing to cooperate, but he needed protection. I watched the group work the issue. Haj Abdul Wahid would slap the table, demanding that the tests be done under threat of arrest while others urged caution and understanding, all in voices whose volume went up and down in the heated discussion. It didn't matter whether the particular issue affected your department or not. This was a type of council of elders, and they were all going to have their say. The conversation went around the table from person to person, each putting out ideas. Col. Hanif, always the practical one, put out the idea that each family elder should be brought forward and told, before the doctor announced his findings, that the doctor belonged to the community because he was treating the people of the community. As such, the doctor was under the protection of the community, which meant his office, the courts, and prosecutors, and if any harm came to the doctor, then it would be assumed that the harm was done by the family that the doctor's finding went against. He would therefore arrest that family's elders and charge them with the crime. The group, after much further discussion, and to the relief of the doctor, liked that idea.

Then, before they voted, Haj Abdul Wahid Acheckzai turned and, looking at me with his hand outstretched in my direction, said, "We should ask our guest, the PRT rule of law advisor, if he has any thoughts." Haji Wahid was not a legally educated man, and he would often ask me about legal theory. I had been sitting as far back from the table as possible, wanting the shura to be theirs and theirs alone. Facilitate the shura but don't get involved was my original intention. It had to be their ideas they would be championing. I had learned long ago people follow what they own, not what you want them to. I knew by the hand gesture that Acheckzai was addressing me, but I used the time it took to translate his words to recheck my notes taken as my translator whispered in my ear what was being said for the past hour. Once the translation was complete, I took a long pause, looking around the room at all the bearded faces looking at me. When I spoke, I validated Acheckzai's assertion that there should be consequences for failure to do your duty under the law; however, there should, as Col Hanif pointed out, be consequences for hindering public officials from doing their duties. I also pointed out that threats against one of them were threats against all of them, and it would be prudent to act together as a group to ensure the group's safety. I had only one suggestion. I suggested that when the doctor took the X-ray that two elders, one from each family, should not only witness the procedure but also that they be shown what to look for on the X-ray. Educate them enough so that they could be confident that the test was valid and conducted properly. This would reduce accusations of favoritism toward one family or the other. The idea was acknowledged, and they agreed that Col. Hanif's approach would be incorporated into the age validation process. As to the young man who had already been in jail two years awaiting his age to be determined, he was tried as an adult, sentenced to two years, and released.

Impact of Education Efforts

The same issue would come around three months later at a legal shura in late May. However, by that time, several events had changed the dynamics of the group. I was able to get a US State Department-INL three-day training seminar from the Justice Sector Support Program (JSSP) into Tarin Kowt. The Afghan attorney general's office (AGO) had sent a new, well-educated chief prosecutor and a team of several young, legally educated assistants. Richelle had been successful in bringing in an NGO, International Legal Fund-Afghanistan (ALF-A), to set up a public defender office. A lawyer from that NGO had come down to establish an office, so he was in attendance. The combination of those events produced a dramatic change in the discussion at this legal shura.

The JSSP traveling seminars had only come into existence a few months before. Even though it was now ten years since the United States had come to Uruzgan and five since the NATO/ISAF organizations had taken over, those in the justice sector, up until May 2011, had little or no legal education. MMJ had been educated years ago within the sharia law faculty of Kandahar University. He had gone on to study Islamic science and was well read otherwise. All others, at best, were university educated but not in any kind of law or legal theory. The JSSP had set up a college-like rotating legal-training program in several major cities, Kabul and Kandahar included, that lasted two months. It was a based on teaching the new Afghan Constitution, the criminal and civil laws that flowed from it, and the procedural requirements that flowed from those laws. It ran into many problems, the least of which was the time commitment needed to attend. Most of the justice sector personnel couldn't afford to leave their positions and other duties for that much time. Also, the attendees had to find a place to live and be able to cover their costs of lodging and food. Pay was so sporadic that this was problematic. So many of the field personnel, such as myself, pushed for a program that would travel out to the rural areas to provide two- to three-day seminars that over time would cover the entire eight weeks provided at one of the regional training centers. The fact was that there wasn't an operational training center in each and every major city running the program every two months. When I finally was able to convince MMJ to send the Deh Rawud district judge Abdul Wahid to the eight-week course in the late summer of 2012, he had to travel to Bamiyan because Kandahar wasn't available at the time. Wahid had forced MMJ's hand by taking bribes from both parties to the litigation, and they wanted to kill him. We needed to get him out of Deh Rawud for his own safety. When he got there, the instruction was in Dari, and he was a Pashtu speaker, so he left. He wouldn't go back to Deh Rawud until the spring of 2013 when he returned with two new, well-educated judges who had been staying in Tarin Kowt for about two years until Deh Rawud was safe enough for them to stay there.

JSSP human rights training at Tarin Kowt
provincial administration building

The programs were designed to be a full three days, but the logistics of bringing them to this rural area proved cumbersome and sometimes a completely exhausting event. The ever-shifting regulations concerning Afghan nationals staying on the base created the most troublesome issue. It would consume hours of our time going from the base mayor to base security to base badging each time the mix of US JSSP advisors and Afghan instructors would come. Most times the training group would arrive in the early morning hours of the first day of training. We would meet them at the flight line and escort them with our badging credentials to the PRT, where the convoy into the PGOV's compound would be waiting. We would get into the compound around 0830 hours and head to the provincial administration building that seemed to be in a perpetual state of construction, where long extension cords lay on the dirty floors and the only functioning toilet suffered from an extreme lack of hygiene attention. The deputy governor had his office there, and more than once we would show up—after confirming the date and time with him several times over—to find him in an absolute uproar over how he had no idea we were coming. This impacted the arrangements for the lunch food that he was in charge of. His display was usually over our insistence that attendees be limited to the formal justice actors while he wished to pack the room with tribal elders and others so they could receive the daily stipend that was given to attendees from outside Tarin Kowt to compensate them for their travel and lodging. He would calm down when I came into the room, and he would take me to his office, where we would once again go through the routine. He would be allowed to save face, and we would negotiate a slightly higher price for the food due to the "short notice." It was an Afghan ritual that we were prepared for, and after the first time, I slipped in certain things, like extra phone calls, ahead of time to bring these negotiations to a quick close.

JSSP trainer getting in a little cricket on an afternoon break

Over the years, I had two Australian Special Forces colleagues, Shane and Trent, who at different times headed up the TF-66 Rule of Law Cell. I brought them into these trainings as they brought the PRT into theirs. It was a great relationship we both were able to leverage well. We would remain outside the room where the classes were held and sometimes walked around the PGOV compound to pass the time. It was an opportunity to watch the comings and goings of different groups who petitioned the governor as well as to talk to the soldiers who guarded the compound. Most times it would be an uneventful day. However, there was the day a grenade was thrown over the wall, and another when MK delivered a small herd of about ten sheep to the new PGOV.

MK's gift of a small herd of lambs to the new
PGOV, Ackanzada, April 2012

We watched from atop the building as the "fresh" meal was herded into the inner compound, where several sheep would be slaughtered for the evening meal being prepared. During the cold winter months, we sought a seat outside to sit in the warmth of the sun. There was always the concern about snipers but not so much that we didn't take advantage of getting warm. Life is raw and basic in Uruzgan.

Fresh lamb for the new PGOV's welcoming dinner

One of the basic dynamics at play in Uruzgan was the sense by the people that the government was acting in an un-Islamic manner. Therefore, I always talked with the instructors before the trainings to explain that they needed to connect the constitution to the base it stood upon, Hanifi sharia. Back in 1786, the British were so perplexed by Islamic jurisprudence they encountered in India that they established something similar. It was Anglo-Muhammadan law based on Hanifi texts. They brought some willing muftis to sit with British magistrates to administer the process. It was a huge failure because it led to claims that the British were attempting to rewrite the laws of God. This Anglo-Muhammadan law was seen as forcing Muslims off the righteous path toward salvation and therefore out of the Abode of Islam. This then triggered the only response demanded by a true Muslim, the Abode of War. Years of conflict followed. Uruzgan, Afghanistan, with its low education and subsistence life was not about to follow anything but proper sharia. Getting the JSSP instructors to teach from a Hanifi sharia base was critical to the acceptance of the constitutional structure by the community. This had a great effect, demonstrated by the conversations later at the legal shuras. The conversation around any issue would include a hearty debate blended with Hanifi sharia and constitutional-derived perspectives, blending the two into "proper sharia." That connection raised the level of debate to where the sharia-trained Uruzganis felt they had a grasp of the secular legal concepts involved in applying the laws developed under the Afghan Constitution.

Watching the cricket match from the warmth of the sunny balcony

Respected faculty members from Kabul University taught these courses. They would come dressed in their suits and ties and provided a stark contrast to the traditional Pashtu dress. We encouraged the instructors to stay at the PGOV's compound with its rather modest and rural accommodations, rather than on the base, so that personal relationships could develop. It was amazing to see the difference between those trainers who embraced that concept and those that didn't. Some complained bitterly about the accommodations, and others did not. One time I became so enraged at one who was loudly complaining that it was humiliating to be placed in such humble accommodations and eat such simple food for every meal that I couldn't contain myself. He spoke English, so I let him have it. I spoke of how these rural peasant conditions he was complaining about were the best in the province. I said I was insulted that he would speak in such a way toward genuinely held-out hospitality that Afghan Islam demanded toward a guest. I had come to really love the Uruzgan people by that time, and his elitist Kabul demeanor had greatly offended me. However, on the other hand, most of the instructors embraced the concept, and several specifically asked to come back with each training segment because the simple hospitality was so genuine. They made friends among the Uruzgan justice group, and it showed with each new round of trainings.

Lunch at these events was always a negotiated affair that provided the same fare of fatty mutton, rice with almonds, onions, cucumbers, and large flatbread that served as placemat, napkin, and eating tool, followed by Coke products or bottled water. Tea flowed throughout the day, and we would arrange, when we could, for the PGOV to come and give a grand speech and hand out the certificates for completing the course. I would always say that Uruzgan needed three things—education, education, and education.

MMJ surprised me at the March 2011 JSSP seminar. On the opening day, he came with six new young judges sent to Uruzgan straight out of the Sharia Law Faculty in Kabul. He strode in like a proud father with six new sons to display.

When the JSSP three-day seminar concluded in Tarin Kowt, they disappeared for several months to attend more JSSP judicial training in Kandahar. Each of these new young judges was designated to go out to the outlying districts. However, due to security concerns, that wouldn't become a reality until the spring of 2013, after I had left the province. When they did return to Tarin Kowt, MMJ used them to form the necessary three-judge panels required under Afghan court procedure to hold trials. He was using what he had to his greatest advantage rather than force them out to areas they would just flee from, which happened in Khas Uruzgan in early 2013. That district was still too insecure as of October 2014. I also noticed that at every legal shura after they came, MMJ would have one of the new judges near him whispering in his ear. His legal analysis rose to new heights with these new young judges to advise him. It was in those moments that I saw his wise humility working its magic.

The Dance Begins: Fighting Season 2011 Begins

The April sun was warming the higher altitudes, and the Helmand River was beginning to rise. The winter snows were melting, and the mountain passes would soon open. The new fighting season was beginning, and tensions were rising. I set a day to go into Tarin Kowt to meet with MMJ. I was bringing our PRT engineer to conduct a survey of the roof of the appeals court to get a cost estimate to repair the leakage into the building. The intense sunlight mixed with the thaw and freeze of the winter months made short work of any faulty construction in Uruzgan. There was plenty of that to go around. I knew the CERP funds would soon dry up, and I wanted the infrastructure of the court to be in place before it did. Nothing slows formal justice like a leaky roof, and the court roof was in sad need of repair. It was not only a courthouse but served as the local residence for the six new judges that had come earlier. and they needed a dry place to sleep.

When I arrived at the appeals court, the garden had been planted, and MMJ was still sleeping in his office most nights.

Uruzgan court of appeals

Speaking with the head of his security, his eldest son, Salam, it was clear travel presented the greatest security exposure. Over the last several months, the Combined Team Uruzgan (CTU) command had been given five armored Toyota SUV vehicles. There had been many meetings to discuss who should get one, and I was pushing hard for the chief judge MMJ. I made a simple argument. "Let's count the number of times a local Afghan official has been targeted and let the person with the most assassination attempts get top priority over those who haven't." I informed him of my efforts but also tempered it with a suggestion that he speak with the PGOV concerning his support with the CTU command that he be given one. He was very grateful and merely said, "Inshallah," God willing.

Malavi Mohammad Jan, Hamidullah, Clay Stafford, and the author at the entrance to the provincial appeals court

Salam, MMJ's eldest son

While the PRT engineer was surveying the roof, MMJ and I sat in his office waiting on tea. We shared some small talk about our families' health. Col. Shirazad was now the PCOP, with the corrupt Juma Gul being transferred to Zabul Province. There was great ironic humor in that move because Zabul PRT had pushed hard to have the former Zabul PCOP removed from his position due to his corruption, just to have him replaced by an even more corrupt individual. I noted that blunder and was a strong opponent to us interfering with their placements. Work with the devil you know rather than the one you don't. However, I was glad to see Juma gone because of his refusal to work with the other justice sector actors such as MMJ. I was hopeful the more "professional" PCOP Shirazad would step up and protect the judges and prosecutors. I would be sadly disappointed.

The good news was an inspection team had come from the Afghan Supreme Court to review the performance of the Uruzgan courts. This was the first time Kabul had reached down to form a connection between the supreme court and Uruzgan courts. It was a start even though the final report from the inspection was critical of MJ's political involvements and the seemingly overpraising of Haji Abdul Wahid, the primary court chief judge, known to me as being corrupt.

What was most interesting at this meeting was MMJ's questioning of me as to the reason behind our failure to defeat the Taliban in the nearly ten years we had been in Afghanistan when it only took us four to defeat Nazi Germany. He was testing me, and my response would cause him to smile and then grow serious. I asked him if it seemed prudent to set an entire farm on fire, killing all the sheep, goats, donkeys, and the families in the compound just to kill the rats we know live within that farm. He stated to me it did seem excessive to do such a thing and it would threaten the entire village. I went on to tell him that the approach of the Allies in World War II was just such an approach. In our efforts to have Adolf Hitler and his Nazi Party surrender, we fired bombed Hamburg with such ferocity that Hitler forbade anyone from leaving the area for fear that the citizens of Germany would seek surrender immediately. I told him I wasn't sure of the exact casualty figure, but I knew it to be in the range of thousands of civilian deaths. I went on to relate similar activities and results in other German cities as well as Tokyo, Japan, not to mention the atomic bombs dropped on Nagasaki and Hiroshima. He knew full well those names, but he wasn't familiar with the German cities I had mentioned. I told him the one thing that concerned me was we would do the same here in Afghanistan if the violence that came to the United States and Europe from here came once again after we left. I felt the Afghan people, through their government, were wasting a God-given moment in a time when the entire world had come to help them by squandering the donor money by putting it in their own pockets and not those of the people. I ended with an apocalyptic concern that if the Western world ever returned to revenge another 9/11 event that we would come with the same vengeance that we went after Germany with in WWII. I said WWII was just the finish of WWI where Germany, as the Taliban had here, negotiated a peace, just to start back to war thirteen years later. I said my children or grandchildren would see no value in sparing the civilian population of Afghanistan from such total devastation. I feared that should another conflict come about in their time, that Afghanistan would share a similar fate. I told him the economics of the West had changed drastically from 2003 to 2011 and that we could not afford to stay with the massive aid that we were delivering now. The Afghans needed to get control of the violence that came from the Taliban and unite the region in peace.

MMJ stroked his beard with his right hand and leaned to his left in total silence for a while. When he did speak, he spoke of outsiders coming to get rich off the backs of the people of Uruzgan. He said that the Pakistanis were the real problem in that they were constantly stirring up trouble in the region to avoid the issue of "Pashtunistan." He said, "Uruzgan needs to be run by persons from Uruzgan," not some outside person who is only interested in making money. I agreed and asked him if the tribes of Uruzgan could stop fighting amongst themselves in an effort to make that happen. He told me he was talking to the elders of the province from all tribes.

I turned the subject to the efforts to increase security around him and the other judges. Sadly, the new PCOP didn't seem any more eager to increase the judicial protection beyond the meager numbers of police now guarding them. I asked him if he had reached out to MK for help, to which he responded with a surprising question of his own. "Jafar, what do you think of MK?"   I recall sitting back with my tea and feeling the warm sun on my face in the cool April air. I looked out into the yard at the dust blowing in the wind. Seeing a small dust devil begin to dance across the front of the courthouse, I took a deep breath and turned to MMJ and said, "The history of all regions in conflict have their own versions of MK, the one willing to fight and having the power behind him to do so. They come and go, and as the Christian book says, 'He who lives by the sword shall die by the sword.' So the question is, does MK want to continue to live by the sword or does he want to be more? Can he make the transition from warlord to statesman? That is the question. First he must have the desire to do so. That would be a good question to ask him the next time you see him. Then the question is, if he desires to do so, is he willing to do what it takes to make that transition? That is the test. I believe if he does wish to make the effort, he must seek the council of all the graybeards of all the tribes of Uruzgan." I went on to tell MMJ the story of the American Indian confederations formed by the Iroquois tribes and later among tribes that followed the great Native American Shawnee war chief Tecumseh. I spoke of how the Iroquois tribes would demonstrate their strength using arrows. One arrow is easily broken but not seven held together. However, the failure of all the tribes to cooperate in a united front would doom them to be conquered by the Europeans. That was a fate waiting on the tribes of Uruzgan by those that would divide them in order to conquer them. Especially the Iranians and Pakistanis. I felt they had no worries about us staying because I knew we weren't, in large numbers, even if our governments reached a status of forces agreement, which I doubted. Then I repeated my mantra that a million eyes and ears attached to hearts that have a reason to see you live are better protection than ten thousand rifles could bring. MMJ said he would think on what we talked about as we rose and embraced each other again.

Osama Bin Laden Is Dead: Please Do the Same to Mullah Omar

It had been a few weeks since our last meeting. It was May 5, 2011, and the picture and face on the front page of *Stars and Stripes* said it all. Bin Laden was at last dead.

Stars and Stripes cover, May 3, 2011

MMJ was "Glad from God Osama is dead" and said, "Mullah Omar needs the same treatment." MMJ was not one to mince his words concerning Mullah Omar and his "wrong sharia" and the Pakistanis that support him. He also stated to me that the new PGOV wasn't serious about bringing Uruzgan forward. That he was "given the province to play it for money." MMJ also confided in me that the Taliban wanted him dead because he was "a pillar of Uruzgan" and an educated person speaking against them. You could tell he was fired up over the killing of bin Laden. I felt he had a new hope for Uruzgan.

Deh Rawud Spring 2011: Farmers, Vampires, and "Chopper"

Uruzgan PRT had three main locations from which it operated. The capital of Tarin Kowt and the districts of Deh Rawud, and Chora. Deh Rawud and Chora were the district centers for the two most populated districts of Uruzgan outside of the capital. The region outside Chora was always sliding in and out of Taliban control, and the city itself wasn't very secure. Rumors and many facts pointed to the Afghan Army units in the area having a deal with the Taliban where they avoided each

111

other. This left the ANP under heavy pressure of attack and a major friction point between the provincial ANA commander and Matiullah Khan. The ANA commander was finally removed in late 2012.

Deh Rawud was a different story. While Chora was more toward the mountains, Deh Rawud had roots in both Helmand and Uruzgan Provinces. The region produced both marijuana and opium poppy, and the routes down to Kandahar and over into Helmand ran through it. The region was contested in some areas, but much was solidly in the control of a flamboyant, young, and charming ANA commander who sported a gold-plated AK-47, Omar Khan. Omar had been a cook for the US Special Forces units that came to the region in 2002 with Hamid Karzai. His willingness to chase down the Taliban led him to the top of the then local militia that was later turned into ANP units. His broad smile and flashing eyes belayed the firm hand he had on the region's opium and marijuana trade, which translated into power. He was in control, and the others followed suit. In the spring of 2011, I made my way there for the first time to speak with him concerning how he viewed policing and using the prosecutor's office as the proper channel to deal with local crimes.

Deh Rawud was not unknown to me. I knew the leader of the Taliban, Mullah Omar, had grown up in Deh Rawud under the strict hand of his uncle and stepfather who was a local mullah. My PRT team leader in Iraq, Linda, had served in the region prior to coming to Iraq. She had shared a few stories of the region with me then. Those conversations had been prompted by the death of her friend and colleague who worked in the area of human terrain studies, much the same as Banger was doing. However, unlike Banger, Linda's colleague was a woman, and that in and of itself didn't sit well in this remote rural region. While having a conversation with an elder male in his home, he took offense to something she said. He got up and threw a pot of hot cooking oil on her. She languished for a year before succumbing to her injuries. Linda was no fan of the region. I reached back to her after my visit to Deh Rawud. I told her that I felt that while walking through the towns of Deh Rawud and Tarin Kowt I was in a bad B horror movie. Specifically, I stated, "It's like one of those movies where the stranger is walking through the town. People are smiling at him and being kind, but what the stranger doesn't realize is that they are all vampires. That they are making the stranger feel welcomed, knowing they are going to kill him when he least expects it."

Her reply was simple. "Yes, they are all vampires." The cultural difference at that time was so palatable, in an uncomfortable way, that I knew I had work to do to understand the culture better in order to accomplish any stability in rule of law. This undercurrent of violence in all things was unnerving to the point that I could feel myself being pushed in a spiritual undercurrent of accepting my own death as a forgone conclusion. That letting go of life was the only way to successfully move forward with what needed to be done Uruzgan. Having studied the Asian martial arts for thirty years, I was truly coming to that point often written about by the old samurai masters. "Accept that you are already dead, and you will pass through combat alive to fight another day."

On this trip to Deh Rawud in May 2011, we would travel by convoy to take in a village meeting outside of Deh Rawud and survey a possible bridge across the Helmed River. The plan was to arrive at Camp Hadrian late in the day.

My gear was stowed on top of the lead Bushmaster as we rolled along the hard dirt road toward Deh Rawud. Several hours later, we detoured along the Helmed River heading toward our village meeting. Listening to the chatter over the intercom, I could feel the Bushie slow to a crawl, and shortly thereafter the grinding sound high on the starboard side signaled a complete stop. The next minutes were tense and seemed to last a long time. Then there came an urgent order to dismount the Bushie. "Now!" I broke open the rear hatch, taking only my "grab bag" loaded with some water, protein bars, 911 GPS, and my notebook, exiting to several Diggers with their weapons pointing toward the opposite tree-covered riverbank a hundred meters or so across the river. With a wall of stone towering over us on our left and the clear line of sight to the tree line, I knew we were in a clear killing zone, and we had to move and move now! I turned to see the Bushie I had just exited teetering on the edge of a ten-foot-high riverbank. So much for the village meeting.

Exiting, I could see our way out was blocked by another Bushie that was attempting to back out of the precarious position. I crouched down low to minimize my profile against the sheer wall to my left while waiting for the path out to be cleared. We were sitting ducks, and the opposite shore wasn't friendly to our forces. What was probably ten minutes or so seemed like an hour.

Our way out blocked for the moment

When the Bushie finally cleared the wall, we covered the six hundred yards or so of ground back to the remaining vehicles as quickly as possible. Clearing the sheer wall to my left was a great relief, for if we did come under fire, I at least had some areas to dive into to seek cover.

Walking our way out along the Helmand

Reaching the other Bushies, we mounted up, and we split up, leaving a guard detachment covering the stranded vehicle while we pulled back away from the river to await additional troops to secure the area before we returned to Camp Hadrian. We set in next to a large hill that was marked on the map as Alexander Hill. Walking to the top with the PRT commander, we had a tremendous view of the valley. The hill received the name due to the ruins that sat on top of the hill. The locals stated that the ruins were the foundation of a garrison held by Alexander the Great. I looked upon the site of the ruins and thought this would have been a strategic position for him to control the valley.

Alexander Hill

You could imagine his soldiers sitting there, and I wondered what they would have thought about these lands so far from their own homes in their time. I wondered if much about this place had changed since then. The vehicle recovery operation would stretch over two weeks. They would have to build a temporary road under the port side of the vehicle to drive it out of the situation.

We arrived at Camp Hadrian as the sun was setting. I scrounged a couple of sheets and a towel and found a bunk in the bunkhouse that held the forty or so bunks to house the transit visitors to Hadrian. Over the next several days, I met the then district governor (DG) and longtime resident Khalifa Sadat. Sadat, a member of the Bobazai tribe, was a man known for his corrupt ways. He delighted in telling boyhood stories about the now famous Taliban leader, Mullah Omar. "Just Omar back then," he would explain, "and not special in any sense of the word." The DG went on to explain how Omar's uncle was a mullah who ran a conservative madrassa, a religious school. When Omar's father died, his brother, as per Afghan tradition, took in his mother as another wife. The uncle was harsh on him, and it was alleged his mother didn't fare much better. Stories of harsh beatings by the uncle were well told in Deh Rawud. All I could think of was how such familiar stories were told about others who would become famous for their own violent ways when they entered adulthood.

After the meeting with the DG, I met with the flamboyant district police chief, Omar Khan, and it was clear he had no concept about policing in the Western community sense, and he didn't care. I chalked up the meeting as the opening round of discussions to come with him. A chance meeting with him at Camp Ripley a month later confirmed his status as the Afghan warrior in charge of Deh Rawud. There would be a slight power struggle between him as a DCOP and Noorazai leader and Matiullah Khan as the PCOP and Popalzai leader in mid-2012 when Matiullah reassigned him to Chora. When I left Uruzgan in January 2013, he would be Matiullah's security chief along with his gold-plated AK-47.

Camp Hadrian was the forward operating base (FOB) that the PRT operated out of. The US Special Forces camp lay a very short distance away. Walking the grounds of Hadrian took all of about twenty minutes. It was a miniature MNBTK with no runway, just helicopter pads. One couldn't miss the connection to the name of the ancient Hadrian's Wall that separated the Isle of Britain between the wild Celts north of the wall and the civilized Roman conquers to its south. In the center of the camp, sitting on a little knoll, was a very small post exchange (PX) run by the contracting company superior, which also had the DEFAC contracts for Uruzgan and elsewhere in Afghanistan. Next to it was the camp church, and both were made out of container units.

Camp Hadrian chapel

The PX had a wooden deck build out from the door, and just off the edge of that deck sat a big male dog, which is the cousin of the Tibetan mastiff. The Kuchai tribe used these sturdy, rugged mountain dogs to guard their sheep and encampments. They were nothing to mess with and were fiercely loyal. However, Afghans, as with most Muslims, don't see dogs as pets. They are for work or fighting. "Chopper" sat overlooking his domain from that knoll. He was the unit mascot. A previous unit had rescued him when a local man had discarded Chopper because he no longer was able to fight in the pit. His named was derived from his ears and tail being cropped or "chopped" to prepare him for fighting. I spent about four days at Camp Hadrian that spring. Banger was there working the terrain and talking to elders farther out in the valleys carved out by the smaller flows of glacier streams and rivers that converge on the Helmand River near Deh Rawud.

Banger copping some Zs with his favorite teddy bear at
Camp Hadrian

In the evening after dinner, I would spend some time with Chopper, sitting next to him on his perch, an evening cup of tea in hand doing some stargazing. Chopper reminded me of several of the Akitas, a mastiff bred from Japan, that I have shared my life with over the years. The large, quiet dog was a good listener, and being next to him had a calming effect. He was clearly loved by the soldiers, diggers, and sailors on Camp Hadrian.

My time with Chopper that evening was broken off by the arrival of Major "Ash" Gogdon. Ash arrived from the scene of the stranded Bushie with my backpack giving me a change of clothing for the first time in two days. This was very welcome, for the next day I was heading outside the wire to attend a police checkpoint commander's weekly shura with the elders in their areas. It was a community policing technique that transferred well in this rural environment. In major US cities, getting police out of their police cruisers and back on the street meeting the citizens one-on-one had a calming effect in high-crime districts. Attending the shura, we drove across the Helmand and up to the high ground overlooking the Deh Rawud valley. There was a police compound set up on that rise, and it was easy to see why this spot had been chosen with its commanding view of the valley.

Police checkpoint overlooking Deh Rawud

A dog the size of Chopper greeted us as we dismounted our MRAPs. He gave us the once over and walked away to lie in his spot just next to the main gateway into the compound. Many village elders had assembled, but they were waiting on a regional elder by the name of Ibrahim Achundzada who had been driven from the area by the Taliban. He had fled to Kandahar and with stability returning to the area he had just recently returned. I engaged the locals in conversation while waiting for Achundzada to make his appearanc,. One man held a child that was obviously in distress. Limp, emaciated, and weak, the child lay in the cradle of the man's left arm, leaning back with her head facing me. The signs of malnourishment penetrated my soul, with her sunken eyes staring at me. Her father was extremely attentive to her. The medic who was with us asked about her health, and by the father's response, it was clear some diarrhea-inducing illness had taken hold. This was very common in the region where only one in five children will survive past age five. The medic encouraged the father to take her to the hospital in Tarin Kowt even though he knew the distance was great for such a person. We were pulling back from having the locals come to the coalition medics for treatment to put political pressure on the Afghan central government to push their own medical system out to the rural areas. It was a hard position that had to be taken if the high mortality rate would ever be addressed. Knowing the policy behind the decision didn't make it any easier for us to watch the reality before us.

I switched the subject to how the last harvest had been. I spoke of my own semirural background, growing up across from a farm where corn was the major crop. They spoke of the lack of cool, moist mornings, causing their crops not to come to full potential. It took a while before I realized they were speaking of the poppy harvest. They continued with conversation that back home in Ohio would have been about tomatoes, soybean, or corn. The language and description of weather was the same; just the crop was different. Later, as we spoke of their children attending the local school, it became clear that the children were needed in the field in a manner reminiscent of the early 1900s Midwest farm economy. The elders were very concerned that school was pulling their children away from the farm and therefore endangering their life quality as they aged. Children were the social security safety net. The economy was that basic, and in a land where farming is marginally mechanized, child labor was still a mainstay of production, especially in the labor-intensive opium harvest where each poppy pod needs to be scored and the paste that oozes out scraped and packed by hand. It was a reality lost on many who were working the area of education in Uruzgan. It didn't help that the minister of education representative in Tarin Kowt was extremely corrupt, and little of the money provided for the educational needs of the children was making its way to the schools. Staff salaries were the main targets of the theft in office by the MOE representative, and there was talk that much ended in the PGOV's hand. At that time, it was still Omar Shirazad.

Walking into the police checkpoint for the shura with
Achundzada. The floor area behind the flowers
where the shura rugs waited.

Ibrahim Achundzada arrived in a uniquely decorated, dust-covered
Toyota Avalon with a curtain stretched across the back window. He
was a big man, and all treated him with great respect. Achundzada was
immediately ushered to a nice sun-warmed spot in the area where all
were seated. The ground was covered in rugs for the occasion, and we
were arranged in the traditional, slightly elliptical circle, with Ibrahim
Achundzada at the far end of the ellipse. Trying to get my legs to cross
under me was always a challenge with my knee replacement. As I was
sitting in such humble surroundings, It never escaped me that I was
so privileged to live in a land where worn-out joints were routinely
replaced. Achundzada started the shura with a prayer, and then we got
down to introductions. I asked him a bit about his history, and he, as
all good elder leaders in the region were, had been a mujahedeen against
the communist regime. He claimed to have assisted Hamid Karzai in
his efforts to oust the Taliban from the region, and that is why they
had him targeted.

The main conversation of this shura revolved around both a land
and a water usage issue. It seems that a strip of land between families had
an irrigation ditch running between the properties. The two families

were struggling over who had the right to divert the water and when. There was quite the animated, high-volume discussion going on, and I was only catching a few translated words. The police mentoring team translator was working overtime. Each party would take turns standing and addressing the group and Achundzada. I could tell things were getting heated, and violence had erupted over this very issue the week before. Achundzada broke the impasse by declaring the group needed to walk the real estate and observe what the situation was. The group associated with the issues got up, and they walked off with Achundzada. We remained behind.

Upon their return, more discussion was held, and the resulting decision wasn't a surprise for us, but I could see that in the win-lose culture of Afghanistan it seemed twisted to those involved. Each side was to have access to the water while one party retained actual ownership of the land the water flowed through. No more blockages or diversions would be tolerated. Now came the tricky part, reducing the agreement to writing. No one there could write, so they turned to the interpreter we were using and asked him to write the agreement down. He was on the spot, and he felt uncomfortable. I queried the group as to who would have the paper after it was written down. They all agreed that several copies of the written agreement needed to be made. I don't know where the carbon paper came from, but suddenly there was enough to make three copies, one for each of the parties and one to be filed with the court in Tarin Kowt. That was at my suggestion in response to Achundzada asking me what needed to be done. Later I would find that often instead of it being filed with the provincial appeals court, the provincial council would keep a copy.

Waiting for the Evergreen taxi at Deh Rawud

I left Camp Hadrian the next day on the RC-S ring route operated by a contractor firm known as Evergreen that operated several civilian-style Huey helicopters baring a distinctive green and white color combination. Maj. Gogdon wouldn't have the Bushie out and back for another week, but the PRT commander, myself, and others had to get back to MNBTK. It was soon time to again sit down with MMJ and discuss how to move the justice sector forward. I was anxious to see if Hamidullah had organized his group for the next legal shura. If he had, then there was a good chance that those working in the formal justice sector, courts and prosecutors, would embrace traditional ways to advance the formal process in Uruzgan. However, before that, I had my own group to grapple with first.

The Joe Ranger

In the Spring of 2011 a former Texas prosecutor was heading up the Rule of Law Section at RC-S in Kandahar. He was working for the International Narcotics and Law Enforcement Division of the Department of State, and he was focused on doing things by the law. That meant the international norms way and not Afghan ways. Midwestern boys learn from an early age, Texans have an exaggerated sense of themselves. Joe, as capable of a prosecutor as he is, rubbed me that way. I had dodged the bullet of going to Kandahar Air Field (KAF) when I first came to Afghanistan and therefore wasn't tainted with its sense of glory. Joe enjoyed the fast pace of being in the military commands "battle rhythm" of meetings and meetings and meetings, all looking for predefined metrics of success based at that time on the number of prosecutors, judges, and buildings to house them. Joe had drunk the Kool-Aid pushed by the embassy and military that we had a better system of law and legal systems to offer the Afghans, and we had a timeline to implement that system regardless of how they felt. This was reflected in the conversations at the Rule of Law Conference later in the year in Kabul where the army major scolded me concerning my assertion that I knew more than General Petraeus concerning this particular subject. I first met Joe at a February KAF PRT meeting. We discussed MK, and Joe had taken the position that he needed to be contained and somehow prosecuted. It was an INL pattern of thought. That thought would be an absolute truth in Chicago or Dallas but not in touch with the reality in Uruzgan, and I told him so. Joe did listen to my cultural approach and gave it some thought at the time; some but not much. I knew my age played a role in my approach, but Joe needed to run his head into the wall a few more times in order to catch up with me. Joe worked in the familiar, as did many, and had a hard time seeing similar legal concepts working in different contexts of an unfamiliar culture. Mostly I think he felt time pressure to show progress in a culture that had no concept of Western time. Most Uruzganis I met knew only that they were born in a particular season when some event took place, not a day, month, or year. The concept of Western criminal procedure deadlines, speedy trials, and set prison terms just didn't fit their concept of time. Reconciliation was the goal of justice in their culture and that took time and a lot of conversation.

Joe and I represented two diverse groups in the rule of law arena within ISAF. One looked at the traditional justice mechanisms the rural Afghans were using and thought we should embrace those as the procedural means to bring substantive changes in rural justice. Then try to tie those traditional tribal elder shuras to the more formal court system. I came away with a sense that we two rams had spent too much time butting our heads together. I knew there was no changing him, and he certainly wasn't in a position to influence me way out in the mountains north of Kandahar. It was frustrating though because it kept me from bringing in the USAID rule of law informal program into Uruzgan. It would take Richelle, "the bee charmer," to work her magic through the Australian embassy to make that happen. I would return to the mountains feeling more and more of the pull of the slower pace of Uruzgan. The poppies were harvested. The sun was once again beating down on the high-level plateaus of Uruzgan, generating the atmospheric dynamics needed for the dust to once again dance high into the sky. It was opening day of the Taliban's declared fighting season.

Traditional Justice Mixed with the Formal: Can We Trust Each Other?

Over the next two months, I would receive mixed messages from MMJ concerning how justice was operating in the Tarin Kowt bowl of Uruzgan. The outlying areas of Deh Rawud, Khas Uruzgan, and Chora were a mix of tribal elders and Taliban justice. I knew MMJ was communicating with the tribal elders in the province as a religious elder but wasn't sure what role was being played as the chief provincial judge, though I couldn't imagine he didn't use that as a leverage in his discussions. My first breakthrough came when I attended the ishula shura. The "ishula" or "peace" shura met every week in MK's compound. Many of its members went to Kandahar for USAID informal justice training aimed at such shuras so they would be educated in proper Hanifi Sharia and its connection to the Afghan Constitution. They were also trained in dispute resolution and how to put together women's "spinster" shuras. I learned from USAID that many of those listed as Uruzgan elders attending their training, which I couldn't bring to Uruzgan, were from this ishula shura group. People sought it out, and MK had his ANP or KAU enforce the rulings. MK was becoming a parallel government in Uruzgan, complete with his own justice system. Seeing he was already on that path, Richelle and I started to develop a strategy to guide it in a more inclusive pattern, bringing the formal court into the picture along with the shura and bringing the USAID education to the non-MK aligned elders in an effort to strengthen the idea of a dual system but weakening the authority of the one aligned with MK. The trick would be to get MK to see the wisdom of not trying to do it all and to share the justice sector with the other GIRoA justice sector offices.

The KAU compound where the ishula shura met was just down the road from MNBTK. Joel, the Australian who did the main research on the tribes of Uruzgan, was keen to go with me, and I was keen to have him along. He knew most of the players in the area, and sure enough many were there. What was of the most interest to me was their desire to present their education credentials from USAID to validate their credibility. In their enthusiasm, they told me that the case they were hearing came as a referral from both Haji Abdul Wahid and MMJ. That was something I held close to my vest upon my next visit to MMJ. The case itself was very interesting, and I could see the value of a community judgment. A young man had killed another man over an argument that didn't involve the family's honor. That apparently had a great influence as to how the crime was seen by the community. There had also been injuries to the murdered man's brother. The shura had about sixty to a hundred members, all male. After hearing the evidence and the arguments from both sides of the dispute, they split into about six to eight groups. Each group discussed the issue among themselves, and then they, each from a designated spokesman, presented their group's findings of what should be the punishment. Hearing all of the groups, the leaders of the groups then discussed the matter among themselves again, but this time in the presence of four to five mullahs who weighed in on issues of the suggested ruling being in conformity with Islamic sharia. In the end, the accused was found to have committed the crime.

Elder group at MK's ishula shura

His punishment was lifetime banishment from his home village, and his family had to pay 300,000 Pakistani rubies in monetary compensation. Additionally, if any threats were made or action taken against the victim's family, an additional fine of one million AFG (afghanis) would be levied against the offender's family. I thought it was, all in all, a fair if not outdated punishment. Banishment from your village in this rural environment could certainly result in the death of the accused. He would have no family to protect him, and in harsh weather he could certainly face starvation or freezing to death. My interpreter, Salihi, was upset with the findings, and as someone who grew up in the urban regions of Kabul, he just couldn't understand why he wasn't sent to jail or executed. We talked about the other ramifications that I saw. I agreed the accused may end up with a fine life in Kandahar, but he would still risk his life to come visit his family in Uruzgan. You could see the rural, urban dichotomy in play with Salihi's struggle to understand the ruling.

Get Your Programs Here—You Can't Know the Players without One

"Who is on first, What is on second, and I Don't Know is on third," and if we weren't talking about the lives of the people, it would be every bit as humorous as the famous Abbott and Costello baseball monologue, trying to follow all the accusations about corruption each justice actor was throwing out there. The Ministry of Justice Uruzgan director, Sayeed Mohammad Sadat, was credible, for he was well educated and an outsider. It was clear to him that the new police chief, the professional Col. Shirzad, was allowing the shakedown of motorists for the privilege of passing through the ANP checkpoints. Sadat's struggle with his corrupt Huquq director, Abdul Mohammad, to operate properly under his control, revealed the family ties to the criminal appeals judge Hamidullah and the prison director, Bishmullah. Sadat's struggle to get his own ministry to properly fund his office, which operated the Huquq, prison, and juvenile center, left him so exasperated that he commented that without ISAF the people would line up behind either the Taliban or a warlord. That statement stuck with me.

A few short days later, the primary court chief judge, Abdul Wahid Acheckzai, presented to me another piece of the Uruzgan puzzle.

Acheckzai used to be the mayor of Tarin Kowt. When he was fired from that position, MMJ brought him in as the primary court judge. I had assumed they were close, so I was a bit taken aback when I started hearing from Acheckzai accusations of the civil prosecutor, Salihi, being so corrupt that he was a "virus" that would destroy justice and that MMJ was renting out to the ANP the other four houses that the Dutch built to house the families of the judges. Acheckzai was quick to point out the praise he received from the supreme court inspection team and how the report criticized MMJ. A visit to the civil prosecutor brought out that the counter-narcotics lieutenant Hotaki delayed the execution of search warrants, resulting in the drugs being gone when the police arrived. Sahlihi, "the virus," was demanding to go along on each drug raid, which raised the question of why? MMJ and another judge by the name of Kudos were definitely focused on Acheckzai and his son-in-law Abdul Raziq as the main source of corruption, but with several kilos of opium found in MMJ's vehicle by TT-66 at a later date, my definition of corruption was narrowed to "taking from the little guy." MMJ was also implicating the PGOV in schemes to profit from his position and not really care about the province. There wasn't one GIRoA official who someone didn't accuse of having their hand in the cookie jar of the unofficial income in Uruzgan. It was only a matter of how much. I was only concerned with what impact it had on stability because, given our deadlines, to attempt to think past that was the ultimate exercise in futility.

We held another legal Shura on Saturday, May 28, 2011. Friday was the day for prayer at the mosque, so Saturdays were the best days for larger meetings. It was the first one since I had questioned MMJ about whether he wanted them to continue. I had told him straight out that I wasn't going to do something he didn't see a value in pursuing, and I wasn't going to be making the calls. They had to own the shura and give it value. He had asked me to continue them, and I did so on the condition that I would set the date for this one, but after that they had to do so. Hamidullah, the appeals criminal judge, had taken it upon himself to make it an Afghan meeting, with food and tea instead of just tea and sweets as in the past. He worked hard at making it a success, except the extra telephone-calling part, which we did together as we sat waiting for the others. Most came, but again both the PGOV's office and the PCOP's office were conspicuously absent. What was very interesting though was sitting in the room with all those who had privately accused the others of malfeasance, and worse, working together to solve common issues. As frustrated as they all were, as self-serving as some were, they did care about how the group perceived them. As the meeting progressed, it was obvious that the JSSP trainings were raising the conversation levels at the shura, and that was cause for hope. Then just as I was getting settled around the idea that the virus, Salihi, would again be chief civil prosecutor, it was announced that a new chief civil prosecutor would arrive shortly. He was a former school principal by the name of Ghulam Farooq Mustafar who had been at the attorney general's office in Kabul for the past several years. Knowing that the AGO was the most corrupt ministry in Kabul, I couldn't wait to meet him. I asked for another cup of tea. Who's on first?

A Sad Reality

Two soldiers died. It is a simple notation in my notebook for May 30, 2011, Memorial Day. I don't have an annotation as to whether they were Australian or American; it didn't matter. I would attend a ramp ceremony within the week and add to the collection of memorial service programs I kept back in my CHU. I just couldn't throw them away even though to me they were no more than a face in the sea of camouflage uniforms that surrounded me daily. They were still young soldiers, like I had been in Vietnam, and they weren't going home. Unlike Vietnam, where thousands of soldiers died in a month, their caskets marked "reusable container—do not destroy" passing by me on the flight line headed for a cargo plane to be shipped back to "the world," the United States, here it was very personal. Every so often, one, two, or three would lose their lives to an IED, suicide bomber, or much worse—an Afghan policeman or soldier would turn on a coalition soldier and shoot him or her in a moment of vulnerability and then flee.

The Australians would prepare their honored dead at the MNBTK Hospital, and they would be placed in a fine wooded casket. The large converted aircraft hangar that served as the Camp Holland gym was arranged to handle the well-attended service for the fallen soldier or soldiers. The Australian ambassador would come down from Kabul to attend the ceremony. After the service, the casket(s) were shoulder carried out by an honor guard, accompanied by pipers. The casket(s) would be placed on board a military vehicle and slowly driven behind the honor guard and pipers through a corridor of soldiers and civilians that reached from the hanger to the aircraft loading pad, over three-quarters of a mile away, rendering their last respects. The dignitaries and commanding officers followed the vehicle, with the human corridor collapsing in behind them as they passed. The casket was driven out to a waiting Australian Air Force C-130 Hercules, while all of soldiers and civilians formed ranks alongside. The casket(s) was loaded while all waited. When the aircraft engines started to rev up and the aircraft started its slow taxi, the entire formation would render a hand salute and hold it facing the aircraft as it made its turn onto the runway. The formations would shift as they followed the aircraft making its way down the runway. All hands dropped as the wheels left the ground. The multitude would slowly, quietly disband, dispersing back toward their respective camp areas. Many would head for the DEFAC to catch lunch before heading back to their work. The ceremony was mentally exhausting, and I would notice an increased presence at the Camp Holland gym on those evenings.

The US soldiers were flown to Kandahar for the bodies of the honored fallen to be prepared for burial back home. Those remains we placed in a body bag, leaving time only for a quick, respectful, and personal ceremony. At Camp Ripley, the SF casualties were moved so quickly we had time only to say our good-byes as the body bag was respectfully carried on a stretcher onto a C-130, often in the middle of the night. It was a tight group of people on Camp Ripley. Memorial services for the US soldiers were held several days later. These events were very personal, and my heart aches even now as I write this.

Camp Ripley memorial wall of the names of
the fallen, Uruzgan, Afghanistan

It would be those faces that drove me to seek a stability model that the Afghans of Uruzgan would embrace. A soldier's life must stand for a greater meaning, not a political ideal. These soldiers were dying so that some child, some woman unknown to them would have a better life than the one of conflict that had plagued these people for so long. I had to do what I could so that my effort matched their sacrifice.

Camp Holland memorial wall of the names of
the fallen—Uruzgan, Afghanistan

Building a Better Bomb

The judges, ANP, and prosecutors were coming in on the first of June
for training in understanding how IEDs were assembled and how to
exploit the evidence an explosion left behind. Known as CEXC, it
was meant to be a one-day course on how to make an IED in the
morning and hands-on evidence examination in the afternoon. It was
an American that was set to instruct on how the bombs were made. I
suggested to him he may wish to keep it short because the people he
would be teaching probably have built more than a few of the IEDs
he would be referring to. Well, that suggestion fell on deaf ears, and
after two hours of instruction, he asked if there were any questions.
Acheckzai from the primary court raised his hand. The instructor called
on him, and Haji Abdul Wahid proceeded to engage the group about
how each of the devices the instructor had showed them could have
been built better or triggered differently, taking suggestions from the
group as he went. I looked at the instructor and just gave him a shrug
of my shoulders and a smile.

Judges and ANP at the CEXC course

What Are We Going to Do about Matiullah?

The commanders of CTU, a Col. Creighton, as well as the RC-S Command, were looking for a way to neutralize MK to allow the professional PCOP Shirzad to gain a foothold. As noble an idea as that may have seemed, it flew in the face of the historical cultural makeup of this region and most of rural Afghanistan. Even though MK had a harsh history toward tribes outside of his uncle Jan Mohamad Khan's patronage network and the Popalzai tribe in general, he was still a local and therefore a preferred power to that of an outside power, and Col. Shirzad was an outsider. A few weeks after the ishula shura, an opportunity opened up to go to MK's for dinner. The PRT military unit was soon to rotate out, and the Commander had been invited to a farewell dinner at MK's home just across from MNBTK's main gate. The PRT CO at that time was Navy Commander Kosnar. Kosnar was a naval submariner in the mountains of Afghanistan, an irony that wasn't lost on any of us. The CTU commander was going to use the evening as an opportunity to pitch MK on an opportunity to head up a revitalized highway patrol unit, which would take him out of the chain of command of Col. Shirzad. I've always enjoyed being the fly on the wall during conversations that may shape policy, and this was going to be such an attempt. Besides, MK was off limits to all but those who had the CTU commander's approval, and I had made it my mission to get to him regardless of any such nonsense.

Rather than walk the three hundred or so meters to MK's compound, we mounted our trusty MRAPs for the short journey. Not a bad idea because we brought more firepower that way and built-in barricades if needed. Dismounting, we walked the short distance to the entrance of the compound and then past his security guards down the dirt drive to the front of his home. His youngest son, about age ten, joined us for the walk, asking in his best English all the questions he could. I would later learn MK had set him up as a television reporter for his local television news broadcast. This station competed with the local Kabul-TV station with its local Afghan BBC correspondent.

Entering the large, three-storied home we dropped our gear just inside the door outside of the main reception room that was covered in rugs. There was a stairway to the left of the main door that went to the upper level and rooftop. We went to the roof to enjoy watching the sun set over the western mountains. It was a beautiful sight. Soon MK appeared and invited us down to the main reception room where the meal was to be served. I was a new face to him, and when we were introduced, I simply stated I was working with MMJ as an advisor to the judges in building the legal system, which included the police and prosecutors. I gave him a big smile and a nod when I asked quietly what at that time was merely a rhetorical question—when he was expected to be PCOP. He looked at me with his dark eyes and just smiled.

The evening progressed with the large room circled with men and lots of food being passed among us. When the meal ended, our small group and MK adjourned to the roof for tea and conversation. Only this time we sat around a long table with chairs. The CTU and PRT commander sat at the head with MK while I went to the end to listen and converse with an Afghan gentleman who happened to speak English quite well. While the CTU commander was giving his highway commander pitch to MK, I found myself listening to MK's engineer in charge of bridge constructions, among other things. One could tell MK wanted to be what the PCOP mentor Lieutenant Colonel Hefner would refer to as the "emperor of Uruzgan." He was the main strongman with a twist, given his ishula justice shura and now public works, which I knew included a school. It was clear to me all the pieces of a strong justice system, if not more, were within reach. The question that I was asking myself that evening was, how would I get these pieces to come together?

I continued to talk with the engineer while keeping an ear open to the proposal being pitched at the other end. I leaned over to the engineer and told him quietly that I mentored the chief judge of Uruzgan and also worked with those mentoring the police. I told him to tell MK that I often encourage the chief judge to reach out to MK concerning the common good of the people of Uruzgan. That a young man such as MK would find great wisdom among those who are older and well educated and who would like to see a stable peace based on proper Islamic sharia found in the Hanifi sharia, upon which the Afghan Constitution is based. Then I also said to tell MK to "study carefully any proposals he is hearing this night, for what is good for Uruzgan can only be determined by those who live here." He was a bit taken aback, but he did promise to speak to MK about our conversation. MK was watching us closely from his end of the table. I have rarely met someone such a MK. He was constantly scanning the room, watching all things and taking note. When we parted that night, I said to MK I had enjoyed the company of his engineer and I wished him well on his bridge projects and all other ideas he may have concerning the growth of Uruzgan into a safe place to raise a family. He smiled and told me to give my greetings to MMJ when I saw him next. "That," I said, "would be tomorrow."

The Hundred-Year Treaty Has Expired

June 6, the D-Day anniversary of 2011 found me discussing the Durand Treaty that expired in 1993 but that Afghanistan and Pakistan are still disputing today. The Pashtu region that Pakistan calls its North-West Frontier Province, or NWFP, is the region where the Pakistani Taliban reside, but most important, it is a Pashtu region, and the Pashtu want to reunite these tribal lands that would in effect create a Pashtunistan that would take all of southern Afghanistan and then flow upward between Afghanistan and Pakistan to the Chinese border. MMJ was on a role explaining how Pakistan is the main instigator of the troubles in Afghanistan. How Pakistan doesn't want Afghanistan to have close alignments with India and how Russia supports Iran, and China does the same for Pakistan, and the Punjabis, which control the Pakistani military, want Afghanistan to remain in turmoil. The onion that must be peeled away in this region to understand all things that are brewing under the surface would take a lifetime of study, and I was rapidly aging.

I changed the conversation to my dinner at MK's home the night before. I spoke of the engineer I met and asked MMJ if he knew of MK's efforts in infrastructure projects, including the school. He said he had heard of those efforts, and I then asked MMJ what he thought of MK concerning those public works. He was silent for so long that I interjected before he could speak again, stating it seemed he genuinely cared about the province. I also stated that I thought we should invite MK to the next legal shura and asked what MMJ thought of the idea. The silence in the room was thick enough to cut with a knife. Then with an affirmative nodding of his head and a sigh, MMJ stated he would like to meet with MK if it would lead to him connecting with the legal shura and his willingness to engage in solving the justice sector issues. I asked MMJ if he would invite MK to the next legal shura, and he said he would. That shura was three days away, but MK's attendance was a year away, for power in Uruzgan doesn't come to you; you approach it, humbly. I had cracked the ice between this Ghilzai spiritual leader and the hated Popalzai butcher who controlled the raw power in Uruzgan. That crack would soon be blown wide open by their common enemies, the Taliban and outsiders, allowing them both to step closer to each other.

Ready, Set, Rotate

June was absorbed by the new personalities arriving. It was time for the annual rotation of our US military, both CTU and PRT. We were in the middle of the replacement in place, which would be followed by the transfer of authority, better known by the acronym RIP/TOA. These were always dangerous times since the insurgents were always ready to take advantage of the hesitation and lack of ground knowledge a new unit has to work through. Hesitation to shoot allows a suicide bomber to get close enough to kill. This would have deadly consequences when the US police military mentoring team would arrive.

Intermixed with this time were many camp-based activities not only related to the handover but to gathering to celebrate the troops going home. The newly constructed, somewhat of a beach volleyball area provided the opportunity for some great friendly competition between all the multinational units, including a team from the local Afghan Army unit.

The UPRT volleyball team in action, with the Windmill
in the background

The Afghans love the game, but they were notorious for palming the ball. The competition started early, but the temperatures rose into the high 30-degree-Celsius range rather quickly, and the sun was brutal. However, that didn't stop any of the "mad-dogs," of all ranks and status, from going out into the midday sun to battle it out amid cheers, laughter, and plenty of water.

The change of command ceremony occurred on June 15, and an evening farewell dinner was held where all the dignitaries from Tarin Kowt were invited. Now that was an education for the observant.

MNBTK had an outer perimeter guarded by a private Afghan security firm. ISAF soldiers guarded Camp Cole and Holland inside that perimeter. Camp Holland was guarded by a Slovakian unit, which was also part of the PRT, and Camp Cole by the US military. The Special Forces at Camp Ripley, where some of the many US civilians lived, was also guarded by an Afghan civilian-run security firm that gave cause for great concern as time passed and more incidents of Afghan security forces, ANA or ANP, turning on ISAF personnel increased in 2012. The Afghan civilian security firm had a nice compound on that outer ring that contained a beautiful area of grass bordered by shade trees. That is where the evening meal was to be held. I picked up the MMJ and surprisingly Hamidullah, his criminal appeals judge, at the main gate and drove them to the dinner. The governor attended as well as many tribal elders, but not MK.

Many speeches were given, and as the late afternoon drifted, MMJ pulled me aside and told me dinner needed to come soon because the night was not safe to travel through, even in the short distance from the main gate to Tarin Kowt. Dinner was served shortly thereafter, and as the evening gathered, the Afghans started to assemble in an area of the grass facing toward the southwest and Mecca. What happened next was an eye opener. They all waited as MMJ, without a gesture or comment from any in the group, strode over to stand in front of the group with his back toward them, and as he went to his knees to pray, they all followed. The power in Uruzgan was diffused to be sure, and MMJ was part of that power in ways I could only imagine. When the prayers ended, MMJ caught my eye, and I gathered him and Hamidullah into my truck, with many others jumping into the back bed, and we drove to the front gate. With the usual hugs, we parted at the gate as he hurried to the safety of his sons awaiting him.

The last days of June closed out with another legal shura, but this time Hamidullah put it together all by himself. Jan would have been proud to see his initiative taking roots. Neither MMJ nor MK was present; however, all other departments, including a police representative, were. Dr. Stanikzai, from the Afghan International Human Rights Commission (AIHRC), started to take a more central role at this shura. This was the beginning of a way to hand over to the Afghans responsibility for this gathering of Uruzgan justice actors. I would meet with MMJ on July 6, letting him know I would be gone until late in July. We spoke more about the need to have a systematic approach to justice in Uruzgan, and that still required the ANP leadership to get involved with the justice actors in all sectors to establish a common path into the future. As we parted that day, the forces of change were poised to thunderously arrive within days. How much MMJ knew of what was about to happen I can only speculate. However, he played a key role in how the events were shaped once they started.

The Khan Is Dead, Long Live the Khan

Jan Mohammad Khan, the former PGOV of Uruzgan who was forced out when the Dutch came to Uruzgan, had left many enemies behind. However, he was still meddling in the affairs of Uruzgan from his advisory position in Kabul. His nephew MK, who had carried out much of the activities that had created those enemies, was now the local power in Uruzgan but still under his uncle's shadow. The tribes needed to come together, but a debt needed to be paid. MK could not rise further with JMK still alive. The Taliban fighting season was well under way, and it would provide cover for much that July of 2011.

It began on July 17 with a typical Taliban-style attack on JMK's compound in Kabul. A small explosion rocked the early morning hours, followed by a burst of gunfire and a suicide bomber detonating himself inside JMK's compound, killing the notorious former PGOV of Uruzgan and a member of parliament by the name of Hashan Watanwal. The Taliban took responsibility for killing JMK, stating it was punishment for his past ill deeds. The Afghan National Assembly blamed the Pakistani ISI. Others looked to local Uruzgan politics and his unwanted meddling there. It's hard to say just who was responsible, but there was one who stood to gain a great deal by JMK's death, and that was Matiullah Khan. What unfolded over the next several weeks confirmed in my mind that even though the Taliban claimed responsibility, he had a hand in it all, even if only a passive one.

Battle of Tarin Kowt

On July 28, just eleven days after JMK's death, a car drove to a position just short of the main gate of the PGOV's compound and waited. Turning off the engine, the man sat in the early morning daybreak hours, probably taking a moment to enjoy the last sunrise he would ever see. At the appointed time, he turned the ignition key to the start position. To his surprise, the engine struggled to start. He tried again and again, and the battery just gave out. He hurriedly exited the Toyota and started to push it. Sadly, and with a naïve trust, the local pharmacist and several young schoolboys ran over to help the man push start his car. However, as he steered it toward the gate of the PGOV's compound, the guards challenged him. He suddenly stopped and in a panic detonated the explosive charge inside the car. In an instant, several innocent lives were blown into oblivion. The attack had begun. Another car was blown on the west wall of the PGOV's compound across from the hospital and just down from the old prison we had walked to just a few months before. Taliban fighters rushed through that breach. The car explosion at the main gate had not breached it, but several Taliban fighters now rushed the main gate. The local broadcast station near MNBTK also came under attack. It was quickly occupied by Taliban fighters and just as quickly surrounded by Afghan police under the command of MK. The broadcast station was close to his compound. The Taliban fighters who entered the PGOV compound from the breached wall by the hospital engaged in a fierce firefight with the defenders. They took the deputy PGOV's office building. He and his bodyguards had fled up the stairs to the roof, where they were trapped.

Deputy PGOV building after the July 2011 attack

A CTU response team from MNBTK was quickly in the fight. When the dust settled, the Taliban fighters were dead, as were several locals who were caught in the middle. Most notably was the local Afghan who reported for the BBC who was caught in the crossfire at the broadcast station. He was well known and liked by the civilian UPRT members. It was a tragic loss for all.

Shortly thereafter, MMJ took two other tribal elders with him to meet with President Hamid Karzai in Kabul.

"Responsible Even for the Dogs"

I was home on R&R when battle broke loose in Tarin Kowt. I wouldn't arrive back at KAF until August 4, 2011 and it would take me three days to get a helicopter flight back to Tarin Kowt, arriving to the celebratory gunfire upon the announcement of MK's appointment as the new PCOP. The flight delays were due to the hot winds that drove the fine powdered "moon dust" into the air. Walking during the hot summer months in Kandahar, one would watch as each footfall fell into this light brown powder of soil that went "poof" around your boots as it rose into the air. It was a deadly mix that chewed up chopper blades, blinded the pilots, and made for long, exhausting waits with your gear, hoping the air would clear. An Australian colleague and folk singer, Fred Smith, produced an album of songs titled *The Dust of Uruzgan*, where he captures the essence of this dust and its intrusive, negative impact on operations.

While there I met with Joe, and he filled me in on the attack in Tarin Kowt and introduced me to his replacement, a former Arkansas judge by the name of Keith Wood. Keith sported a gray beard similar to mine, and we hit it off from the beginning. Judges have heard it all, and his laid-back Alabama attitude fit this region of Afghanistan. I would have Keith as my guest on a few occasions in Tarin Kowt.

Keith and the author outside of MK's ishula shura

Once I did get back to Tarin Kowt, I was anxious to make contact with MMJ. That didn't happen, as he had gone to Kabul. It was mystery to me as to how he could get to Kabul without me hearing one word about it beforehand. Land travel to Kabul was dangerous, so I would often get a request to put someone on our US Embassy Air flights, but not him.

Richelle had set up a meeting with the public defender the Australian Aid organization had funded through International Legal Foundation Afghan (ILFA), Gul Rahman. Gul was a godsend to the region's justice sector. His higher education raised the bar within the justice sector in Uruzgan. He was a humble man and never insulted any of the local, less educated people within the justice sector. That was in stark contrast to the new chief civil prosecutor and MOJ director, Sadat, who managed to alienate most of them. Gul laid out a clear picture of the corruption in the civil prosecutor and primary court offices where fees for release or a "solution" that allowed a defendant to be released were frustratingly well known to him. The good story was that of the appeals court, seemed to be doing things by the book. The problem was the book stated that three judges were needed for a decision, and getting that quorum was an issue. Uruzgan needed more judges, and nobody had seen the six new young judges since they left for Kandahar back before the fighting season opened in late May. Security was still the main issue to get judges to come and stay in Uruzgan.

The following day, we had a meeting with the United Nations Assistance Mission Afghanistan (UNAMA) rule of law representative Khushal Safir. He indicated that MMJ was working with MK's shura and that MMJ left for Kabul after the attack on the PGOV's compound via MK's protected convoy to Kandahar. That answered the question as to how MMJ was getting to Kabul. Now I needed to know what hand he played in getting MK appointed PCOP. The onionskin was slowly, painfully peeling away. A few days later, it was announced that the PGOV Omar Sharizad would be leaving his post in just a few short weeks, right after Ramadan. I had a meeting set with MMJ for August 18, and I was anxious to hear what he had to say about the turmoil of the July events.

Entering the appeals court compound that hot August morning, the first thing I noticed was the increased security and a new armored SUV that the Combined Team Uruzgan commander had delivered. MMJ greeted me at the entrance of the court with a warm Afghan greeting that included much hugging and hand holding. In an appreciative manner, he began thanking me for the new vehicle. This would allow him to safely travel from his home and the court, not to mention other elder meetings in the area. We went into his office, and as the tea was brought in, I asked about the new security personnel in the compound. He began with telling me about his trip to Kabul to meet with Karzai. He had traveled there just after the July 28 attack on the PGOV's compound. He reminded me that without security there can be no rule of law, and after the attack he felt that the only person capable of delivering that security was Matiullah Khan. So he went to speak with Karzai about making MK Uruzgan's PCOP. I was keenly aware that MMJ stood in opposition to the now assassinated Jan Mohamad Khan. The cruelty JMK was responsible for demanded avengement before the Uruzgan tribes could be at peace. MK had been the target of the local anger with JMK in Kabul. However, it was now a moot point. Things had fallen conveniently into place for MK. More than that, one of MK's local tribal rivals was Mohamad Nabi Khan Tohki. MMJ revealed to me that they were cousins through his great-grandfather. I already knew that the criminal appeals judge Hamidullah was related to MK through MK's marriage to his daughter. The thread of power patronage was revealed further.

MMJ confirmed that the recently appointed PCOP Col. Shirazad was being removed and replaced by MK. However, the discussion around the PGOV Omar Shirazad's replacement took an unexpected twist. MMJ went into his usual speech that outsiders come into Uruzgan not to help it but to take from it. With nothing worth taking other than opium, it wasn't hard to connect those dots. What did surprise me was he stated President Karzai asked him to be PGOV, a position he turned down, stating a provincial governor must worry about all things in the province, even being "responsible for the dogs in the streets." This he did not want to do. I thought this was something he didn't have to do, for I could see that he was a master chess player, and he had just established the advantage over his enemies without needlessly exposing himself. Within a year, I would hear the words "the most powerful man in Uruzgan" being applied to MMJ. However, he wasn't quite there yet. The game had a few more moves to be played before this quite unassuming man would claim that title. MMJ was keeping all eyes on MK and therefore keeping the eyes off of him. He was a classic backroom power broker.

I left that day reminding MMJ that MK's greatest challenge would now lie in how he proceeded as a community leader. Would he administer his police through force upon, or by the consent of, the people? We spoke of how MK would need to start down the road of being an elder of the community as well as a PCOP. Not just power but wisdom in the use of that power. I said to MMJ, being very straightforward once again, that the wisdom of all the tribal graybeards must be sought out, maybe not followed but sought out, to broaden MK's base of consent in order to bring stability to Uruzgan.

The Emperor of Uruzgan

As the weeks progressed, it became clear that MK was reaching out in ways the previous two PCOPs had not. Whereas before the civil and military prosecutors had no protection or transportation, now they were receiving both. Whereas before police misconduct was left unaddressed, now the ishula shura was hearing complaints, and compensation was being awarded. In a meeting with our PRT director in September, MMJ indicated he was mentoring MK. The attendees at the legal shura in September were enthusiastic and productive. There was a change in the air, and all felt it, even the Taliban.

As the colder weather approached, reports came in that the Taliban fighters had reached out to MK for assurances of safe passage back to Pakistan. The word was he gave them three days to get out of Uruzgan. Now this begged the question of their role in the events of July. In the constant world of alliances and re-alliances that is Afghan tribal politics, the Taliban attack opened the door for MK to be named PCOP. Coincidence? Maybe, but I wouldn't count on it. There was even talk that MK wanted to be PGOV, but LTC. Hefner, the PCOP mentor, continued to laugh that off, stating, "Emperor of Uruzgan, yes, but not PGOV."

In evidence to that statement, several actions on the tribal side of Uruzgan politics unfolded in rapid succession. Jan Mohammad Khan's assassination placed three young tribal leaders eyeing one another for power: Mohammad Doad Khan (MDK), the son of JMK's former rival, Rozi Khan; Mohammad Nabi Khan Toki (MNKT), a relative of the chief judge MMJ; and Qasim, the son of JMK. It was reported that Qasim offered the Popalzai turban to MK. December 2012 found MDK assassinated in Kabul, and there were reports of his assassin being seen shortly thereafter at MK's compound. MNKT retreated to his compound, staying out of MK's way, and Qasim was turbaned as the new leader of the Popalzai in Uruzgan. There was no real investigation of MDK's assassination, just claims that it was, conveniently, the Taliban.

The rule of law team on MNBTK could only move forward with the Afghan players we had and leave the politics alone. It was just how stability is negotiated in Afghanistan, and Karzai himself was yet to make it out of the presidency alive. So we focused on bringing in the European Police (EUPOL) Coordination of Police and Prosecutor and Justice Sector Support (JSSP) training programs as we continued to focus on the Uruzgan justice sector coordinating their efforts to bring about a systematic approach to formal justice in Uruzgan.

Matiullah the Benevolent

September 2011 saw the end of Ramadan, followed by talk about who would replace the soon-to-depart PGOV Omar Sharizad. Whoever would be selected would have to come to some accommodation with MK and hopefully the Uruzgan Justice sector, which was beginning to find its legs in organizing for the betterment of Uruzgan. November 2011 brought the big Eid celebration, and Matiullah was feeling large. He brought in a major Afghan musician and celebrity to entertain the men of Tarin Kowt. My interpreter was highly impressed that such a well-known and celebrated musician would come to Uruzgan, though I failed to record his name. No expense was spared, and a mountain of the faithful came to Matiullah's compound to join in his success.

At Matiullah Khan's Eid celebration, Matiullah's portrait
above that of his uncle Jan Mohammad Khan

The author and the musician with MK and Scotty in
the background

The Myth of Poppy Eradication

The fighting season wrapped up as the Taliban fighters scurried like
rats over the trails back to Pakistan before they got snowed in. The
farmer started to seed his land to take advantage of the spring snow
melts. Pomegranates and almonds abound but don't pay nearly as
well as the poppy with its opium paste production. Poppy is illegal to
plant but punishable by only a fine. Eradication programs involved
bypassing hundreds of hectares (1 hectare = 10,000 square meters) of
land in poppy production to beat down with sticks a single hectare.
Claims of thousands of hectares destroyed were always reported by the
Afghan government, which collected money from donor countries as
an incentive to destroy the crop, only to have satellite imagery prove the
claims to be highly exaggerated after the fact. Sometimes the poppy was
plowed under and supposedly replaced with wheat seed. The problem
is poppy is a weed that will outgrow wheat, and therefore the impact of
plowing the weed under was negligible. As of June 2014, Afghanistan
was set to be on the verge of a huge crop of over six thousand metric

tons of opium. In December 2012, Uruzgan was poised to be a lead producer well into the future. I was just waiting to see whom the PGOV position would be offered to. Whoever it would be would have to have the backing to take on MK, for the only reason an outsider would come here would be to get a cut of the opium trade. The man selected was the brother of the former PGOV of Helmand Province, which lay to the southwest of Uruzgan. His name was Amir Mohammad Achundzada Wardak, a powerful name in Kandahar, and his brother was a known drug lord. The British had petitioned to have his brother removed from his post as governor of Helmand after finding nine metric tons of opium paste in the Helmand PGOV's compound. One strongman sent in to face Uruzgan's strongman with rumors abounding that they were going to work together to maximize the opium trade. Those rumors proved not only wrong but also misplaced. Millions of US dollars were at stake. The next round of Afghan politics was in place in Uruzgan by December 2011, and by February 2014 the conflict between PGOV Achundzada and MK would erupt in a huge public protest and violence, causing both men to be called to Kabul for consultations.

As my first year in Uruzgan came to an end, I was frustratingly close to bringing the justice sector together. The team of TF-66 Rule of Law Cell, the Australian Federal Police, UPRT rule of law, and CTU police mentoring were working well together. Jan's legal shura concept was gaining legs, and EUPOL was yet to play a vital role in bringing a systematic criminal justice approach to Uruzgan. We were waiting on a specially trained US Army police mentoring team to arrive. As I prepared to leave on R&R in mid-December 2012, I knew that the major driver of the economy of Uruzgan, opium, had to be tied to the criminal justice system. The frustration with the international donor money not making it down to the civil systems that served the people of Uruzgan left no other choice. A deal with the devil, but unless the corruption of Afghan officials keeping donor money from reaching the people of Uruzgan could be stopped, it was one that had to be made. Insurgents came from the disenfranchised farmers of Uruzgan. The little guy getting screwed by the system of corruption had nothing to support but those that supported him. Those in control of Uruzgan's wealth had the key to open the door of stability. Would they be open to turning that key? What role would the new PGOV be willing to play? Was he just another outsider who came to steal from the people of Uruzgan? Only time would tell.

Welcome to Tarin Kowt

Thanksgiving 2011 brought a long overdue asset to the US State Department contingent with UPRT in the form of Haris (Ha-rees). He was selected by the US embassy and assigned to us as an Afghan governance advisor.

Well-educated Afghan Pashtu/English speakers were few among the interpreter pool we had to draw from. Earlier in January and February 2011 I had involved myself with teaching English to any of the interpreters who wished to improve their understanding of English. This was a necessary extracurricular activity on my part because my conversations were laced with legal terms that most interpreters didn't understand. Also, slang presented difficulty for them because its use was common among the troops engaged with Afghans, and miscommunication was a problem. An example of that was the use of the word "fuck" and its many variations. It was the word the young Afghan interpreters wanted to know most about because they just didn't understand it. When I first explained its literal meaning, the shocked looked on their faces were followed by hands going to their months. They all sounded like six-year-olds with a "ohhh" escaping from their mouths, and it was so visibly funny to me I couldn't keep from laughing. They laughed right along with me, as young boys do when an uncomfortable sexual revelation is presented in public. Those evenings were full of fun times.

Haris was a well-educated young man in his early twenties who was still in the process of taking his exams in Pakistan. I took him under my wing, getting him situated in his quarters and all his necessary badges, which labeled him as being allowed to enter into our working areas, eating at the DFAC and escorting Afghans from the main gate onto Camp Holland. He was to become an indispensable member of our team.

On one of our trips down to the main gate and the office that was responsible for issuing the badges with photo ID, we were walking along the road, cheerfully talking to each other. We were just about to enter a walkway flanked by short HESCO barriers when the incoming alarm went off. I grabbed him by the nape of his neck and flung us both to the ground. We felt the thud of the impact and the muffled explosion as the rocket slammed into the exterior side of the taller HESCO situated on the other side of the road. This was my second close call near the main gate. The first was a huge explosion of a fuel truck sitting in the quarantine section located just on the other side of the outer road HESCO wall. A suicide bomber on a motorbike hit the truck, probably hoping to breach the wall. I was just heading down the road in that direction when the truck exploded. Fortunately, the HESO held, and I just turned around. On this occasion with Haris, our heads were turned so we were facing each other. I just smiled and said, "Welcome to Tarin Kowt."

A Year of Living Dangerously

January found me returning to Kandahar from a Christmas R&R. Getting on the aircraft to Kabul, which was to stop at MNBTK, the pilot informed me he would try to get me into TK but to not count on it. Climbing into the sun over the mountains north of Kandahar, the Embassy Air flight seemed routine. Then we approached MNBTK and flew into a large cloudbank. The pilot climbed above the clouds, circling the airfield lost in the marshmallow cloud below. He went on the intercom, letting me know he was circling, looking for an opening. I was watching up the aisle through the cockpit window when he suddenly turned hard to the port side in a dive. I could see the opening in the cloudbank he was trying to go through to get under the cloud. MNBTK airfield was a pilot's discretion airfield. That meant it was his call as to whether he felt it was clear enough to land. Even the best airfields in the world would struggle with such white-out conditions, and we were not even close to being in that league. With my stomach pushing up through my throat, I watched as the ground grew closer, knowing the mountain ridges were just outside the vision of the pilot. Then suddenly the cloud engulfed us. The pilot pulled out of the dive, and we both simultaneously said, "Screw that!" So after a statement questioning both his sanity and the legitimacy of his birth, we laughed it off and we were off to Kabul.

Arriving in Kabul late in the afternoon, I went through the usual, "Why are you here? You're not on our list!" routine from the embassy's ground transport facility. I was always glad to not be near the flagpole too often. They were finally convinced that they were obligated to come pick me up and not leave me overnight at the Kabul Airport. Lucky me. Arriving at the embassy compound, similar questions greeted me, along with looks of disbelief that I wasn't in the computerized travel program as having authority to make the travel to Kabul. After a moment of explanation concerning the weather we encountered, I was sent across the way to the luxury of the transit hotel next to the embassy compound. It really was luxury, given the marble floors and hotel-like atmosphere. I was placed in a room with six others, one of who was Stu, our UPRT agricultural advisor, the builder of the Taj Mah Deck. He too had been delayed in getting back to MNBTK, and he had put his time to good use, acquiring his daily limit of beer purchases allowed at the embassy employee store. When he and I finally got out a week later, we had a gorilla box full of beer. We had to make special arrangements for the additional weight, but it was worth it. I was always confused over the military's general order number one, which banned all the pleasures of life, beer among them. In Vietnam, the beer flowed in pallets hung from helicopters. Here you had to smuggle it onto the military bases. The locals were dipping opium at every meeting while our troops had to settle for St. Pauli Girl "near beers."

Stu and I settled in, waiting on each day's flight to MNBTK. The weather kept us on the ground for a few days while on others we made the flight down just to have to turn around again. Stu and I made it to karaoke night at the embassy employee's club named the "Duck and Cover." We found we made a fairly good duet in the area of Eagles and Bob Seger songs. It was during this interlude I learned that Stewart had spent some time in Kabul in his teenage years. His father was involved in setting up the airport in Kabul back in the early 1960s. He spoke of how beautiful and peaceful Kabul was back then. He still carried his old Afghan-issued documents and drew them out as he spoke of walking the streets and being involved in the nightlife "back in the day."

We didn't get out of Kabul until the end of the week. By the time we got on the Embassy Air flight, it was carrying nearly half of the UPRT civilian members coming back from both the United States and Australia. When we landed at MNBTK, the other half was waiting on the ground to leave on their R&Rs. It was nearly the end of January 2012. I didn't know it at the time, but I had one more year left. It was to be a deadly year.

During the time I was trying to fly in from Kabul, several members of the newly arrived US Army police mentoring team were killed by a suicide bomber on their first mission to the Afghan National Police substation in Tarin Kowt. That substation sat next to the civil prosecutor's office where I frequently went for meetings. The toll would rise throughout 2012, with four military colleagues working with the ANP being shot from behind in the head, and several Australian military personnel would be killed when ANA soldiers turned on them. A suicide bomber in Chora just north of Tarin Kowt would seriously injure an Aussie colleague along with a USMC captain I worked with. It would be in July of this year when Taj Mohammad, from the appeals court, would be killed by an IED that was set by his own son. MMJ would constantly be warning me not to trust the ANA on the base because "they are not from Uruzgan, and I can't protect you." Comforting thought that he had extended his protection over me, but a little disconcerting that he feared for my safety on the base that I drove around every night alone and unarmed.

Within days of returning to the States in February 2013, Ann Smedlinghoff would come down to neighboring Zabul Province from the US embassy in Kabul to deliver schoolbooks. She would be the first State Department person to be killed in Afghanistan, when a vehicle-borne IED targeted the MRAP she was traveling in. My former UPRT USAID colleague would be injured in that attack. These deaths and US government sequester of money would combine to pull all the US civilian UPRT members out of Uruzgan a full ten months earlier than we expected. Yes, it was to be a deadly year.

Return to Deh Rawud

Early in February, I was heading back to Camp Hadrian and the town of Deh Rawud for several days. I had worked through the STOF command and the Hadrian UPRT to have a legal shura convened to address the struggle and dysfunction between the district chief of police, Omar Khan, the new district governor, Amanullah Khan Acheckzai, the district prosecutor, Shah Mohammad, and the judge Abdul Wahid, who Omar Khan threatened to kill. This year had a sense of urgency to get the justice sector functioning. The 2014 drawdown was nearing, and time was running out.

Omar Khan was the power in Deh Rawud. He was from the dominant tribe in the region, the Noorazai. He had started his rise to this position by taking great risks. The Taliban were well entrenched in the western region of Uruzgan along the borders of Helmand and Kandahar. US Special Forces were first in the fight there, and Omar went from cook to local militia leader to Afghan police commander. He would patrol with his men, talking to the people along the way. He was well liked by the Noorazai, but he wasn't a uniting force for the area—quite the contrary. In 2012, he was lobbying heavily to be allowed to immigrate to the United States. There was no doubt in my mind he controlled the majority of the opium trade in this area of Uruzgan. He had a cowboy mentality and would brutally suppress any opposition to him. That said, he did reach workable accommodations with the new district governor and the district prosecutor. The local judge, as the new DG would put it, "was an idiot," and Omar didn't tolerate him at all.

Meeting with Deh Rawud Prosecutor Shah Mohammad,
Judge Abdul Wahid, DGOV Amanullah Khan Acheckzai,
and DCOP Omar Khan in February 2012

Arriving by helicopter at Camp Hadrian, the first thing I noticed was Chopper wasn't upon his throne in front of the base PX. More disturbing than that was none of the members of this PRT military contingent had ever seen the big dog. Walking past the church, I noticed it was open, and a typically lanky Aussie Army officer was milling about inside. I poked my head in an met the circuit-riding padre, Martin. He was a joy to talk to, and I found he would be there for a few days to minister to the Australian Mentoring Task Force (MTF) personnel. I promised him I would be back to chat a little longer. What neither of us knew at the time was we would be stuck at Hadrian several days longer than we anticipated.

We started to meet one-on-one with local leaders in the days running up to the Deh Rawud legal shura. It was clear that there were many with complaints about the way Omar Khan was running things in Deh Rawud, and since MK's rise to power at the provincial level, they were reaching out to him to reign in his district chief of police. The new district governor spoke of how good Omar Khan was for the region and that the judge was troublesome due to his incompetence. The people brought their legal matters through the prosecutor either to him or Omar Khan for resolution, bypassing the judge. The new judges who were assigned to Deh Rawud a year ago had shown up to register themselves, and then they left and hadn't been seen since. I told him they were in Tarin Kowt now, just returning from additional educational courses, Ramadan, and EID. I too was disappointed in their failure to get out to Deh Rawud. They cited concerns for their safety, and the DG scoffed at that, saying he would protect them. However, in the same breath, he complained that as an outsider himself, he had difficulties in getting things done in this region. I told him I was in the process of getting Judge Wahid scheduled for the eight-week judge's training in Bahmian, to which he replied that was good because he couldn't do anything now, but this would be his last chance to perform when he returned. The good news in that was at least this new DG was seeking competence in the position whereas the previous one used that to keep the people coming to him, which provided him with a corrupt cash flow. Things were looking up, if ever so slightly.

Meeting with several elders, allegations of land grabs by Omar Khan, the Afghan Local Police commander, Jan Allah, as well as MK's local KAU commander were voiced. The elders were fearful to raise these issues with the government in Tarin Kowt due to death threats. They all agreed Omar Khan was good for security, but after arresting any Talib, they would pay a bribe to him, and he would let them go. So the circle kept spinning, dancing the dust ever higher.

The evening before the big shura at the district governor's compound, just before sundown, I was sitting on the knoll in front of the Deh Rawud PX drinking my tea. I was lost in thought when my eye caught the sight of a big, dirty white dog making his way toward me, with several soldiers looking on. I stood up and smiled and called out to him. "Chopper?" He looked up, and what was left of his tail started wagging. He picked up the pace as he came up to me, settling at my feet. I started scratching his big head with both hands. The soldiers came up to me and asked me what I knew about the dog. Like young boys with a new puppy, several ran to bring him food and water. Chopper looked tired. He had obviously traveled a long way. He and I settled in for a long-overdue one-sided conversation while I delivered a much-appreciated head and ear scratching. The old dog was a good listener as I verbalized my thoughts about how this region of western Uruzgan was one bridge too far to cross in the time frame I knew we were facing. In the United States, both the political will and the economy were against our continued extension this far out into the rural areas of Afghanistan. I didn't know at that time how quickly our involvement in the capital of Tarin Kowt would end. However, on that night, watching the sun set with Chopper lying next to me, I allowed myself to feel the rough beauty of this harsh land flow through me. The people here were good people caught up in very harsh conditions. Chopper was not to escape those harsh conditions. I found out later that week that once we brought our bomb dogs onto Camp Hadrian, the diggers and soldiers of the previous PRT and MTF were ordered to "dispose" of the "animal" or it would be euthanized. Our dogs couldn't be exposed to the risk of any disease Chopper may carry or any dogfight. Never mind they had managed to have him vaccinated and the bomb dogs were always under strict supervision. Their solution was to take him out on their last long-range patrol and drop him at the furthest point away from the camp. They had hoped one of the Kuchi nomad herding tribes would find him and put him to work. His return placed the new PRT and MTF personnel in the sad position of having to follow the order. The cruelty of war has many layers, and Chopper would be just another civilian casualty of the conflict.

Just a Simple Farmer

The day of the Deh Rawud shura had arrived. These meetings were always organized during the winter months, the nonfighting season, to reduce the risk of attack. Much like the Colonial Army under George Washington, the Taliban had to wait for the snow to melt and roads to dry to move into position to attack. They also often had to wait until after the poppy was harvested to field a large enough force to launch any significant raids.

As we gathered around our convoy vehicles, Chopper meandered by to see us off. Both the PRT and the Special Forces vehicles from the nearby Special Ops FOB would be involved in the move. The village stability operations force had reached out to me earlier to get more involved in establishing a functioning criminal justice program in Deh Rawud. A new captain on that team was a police officer back in the States, and it was a good fit. The Australian SAS Task Force 66 had an actual Rule of Law Cell operating alongside the Uruzgan ANP Provincial Response Corps, and this effort by the Army Green Beret unit was using that model to expand their efforts. We were hopeful that a fresh effort could gain traction.

We arrived at the main district government compound that lay across the street from the main mosque. That was always a mixed blessing, walking the line between those who could be outraged by our presence and those who demanded peace at such a location.

Walking past the mosque and over into the government compound, I couldn't help but notice how far back the soldiers had pushed the locals. Once inside the compound, I saw that many local tribal elders had come to the meeting. I dropped my gear and began making the rounds to introduce myself. The district governor, Amanullah Acheckzai, was there but not the district police chief, Omar Khan. The February schedule was well in place. No real face time would occur until the warming sun could shine upon the group sitting on the ground.

Taking the opportunity of this time before all arrived, I went around and introduced myself to the tribal elders and the newly arrived Huquq (Rights) director for the area, Mohammed Sharif. He was a young man fresh out of university who had grown up in the area. He was pleased to show me the new Afghan law books he had received. Well, I thought, at least they had a reference library where both the local population and the local officials could look to when making decisions. DGOV

Acheckzai and I took some time to engage in pleasant conversation while we walked around the compound. He deflected my questions concerning any friction between Omar Khan and the local population by stating he was an outsider to those in Deh Rawud and therefore without power, even though he was the DGOV. He therefore must defer to Omar Khan on most issues of importance. The one thing he was adamant about was the local judge, Abdul Wahid. His incompetent rulings and stupid ways were becoming a huge source of embarrassment. It was here that the DGOV used the phrase "idiot" when speaking of the judge. The DGOV knew of Wahid taking bribes from both parties to a dispute and once going so far as to ask for a man's daughter as payment for a favorable ruling. He was forced to leave town both times for his own safety. I told the DGOV of my efforts to get Wahid to an eight-week course for judges so he could be better trained to do this job. The DGOV said that would be best. When asked about the presence of the other two judges assigned to the area, he just smiled and said they came, they registered so they could collect their salary, and they left. It wouldn't be until mid-2013 that the judges would return.

Lah Mohammad Bobazai, a local elder, struck up a conversation with me, telling me he had been the chairman of his village's district community council, a now-defunct USAID program that attempted to mimic the tribal elder councils that were so decimated under the Taliban. He was a jovial fellow who had been close to the last DGOV Kalifa Sadat, who had been transferred to Chora in an attempt to break his corrupt hold over Deh Rawud. It was the bane of Uruzgan to have so few educated people to draw from in order to fill the necessary government positions; corrupt individuals were just shuffled around to minimize their negative impact. It will be another generation before the ranks of the educated are full enough to just outright dismiss someone. Though it was starting to happen in mid-2013 in a few areas. The patronage networks were also to blame for this practice. Lah Mohammad was the brother to the former Uruzgan provincial chief of police, Juma Gul. The rotund, corrupt former PCOP was now in Kabul after being pulled out of Zabul after less than a year for his corrupt ways. Lah Mohammad started telling me how corrupt Omar Khan was, taking lands and releasing Taliban after they paid a bribe to the DCOP. My mind kept playing the image of Juma Gul and Omar Khan engaged in a fistfight at a shura in Tarin Kowt after exchanging insults and accusations of corruption between them. Lah told me he was fearful to raise these issues with Tarin Kowt because of death threats he had received. Translation, "I want you to raise these issues with the provincial chief judge and prosecutor." One had to be constantly on guard not to be used. Whether the allegations were true or not was impossible for us to tell. However, given his relationships were at odds with Omar's, whatever truth there was in them was not for us to decide and try to enforce. Such a game would have deadly consequences in Khas Uruzgan seven months down the road.

Omar Khan didn't let my stroll with Lah Mohammad go unchallenged when he arrived. Waving at me with his big smile, he came directly toward us as he entered the compound in his ANP uniform and a .45-caliber pistol stuck into his belt. Ever the cowboy with his boyish grin, he reached out to embrace Lah and me. Lah didn't skip a beat and immediately began to joke with Omar as if he had said nothing to me about Omar's shortcomings. Exchanging pleasantries with Omar, I asked him how he saw the events concerning MK and his recent rise to the position of provincial chief of police. His reply was that such things were beyond a simple farmer such as he. Putting my arm around his shoulders, sweeping my free arm and hand across the horizon in a grand gesture while throwing back my head as a full laugh escaped my mouth, I said, "I can see that he was a very good farmer, given all the poppy that was grown in the district." He just smiled and laughed right along with me. I noticed Lah was joining right in. I paused for just a moment and looked straight at him, asking, "How are you going to use that yield to make a better Deh Rawud District?" He just looked puzzled and I knew he was no Matiullah Khan, and the ability to start what I had in Tarin Kowt wasn't in the cards here. Besides, we just didn't have the time.

The shura got off to a fine start. Many fine speeches were made with the "complete idiot," the district judge, getting up and stating that the court needed to be respected. They all agreed, and the district governor pointed out that the judge would soon be going to an eight-week judicial training course that I had arranged. The applause was long and hard.

Circuit-Riding Padre

With the shura wrapped up, I would spend another week at Camp Hadrian waiting for the weather to once again clear sufficiently to allow helicopter transport back to MNBTK. It was at that time I had the pleasure to make the acquaintance of the Episcopal priest, "Padre Marty." An Aussie in his mid-fifties riding the circuit from camp to camp, the padre was providing spiritual services to the troops and other camp occupants. The man was a pleasure to converse with, which proved invaluable as we waited for hours in the cold, day after day, seeking what little warmth the fleeting sun provided, for the helicopter that never came. He was straight out of the scene from the movie *Longest Day* where the British padre, while under fire, kept going back under the water of a stream where he had lost his religious kit until he found it. Dedicated and always smiling, he told me of how he worked the circuit regularly to hold services for, as he put it, the "lads." We continued our visits back at MNBTK where he and other chaplains started a program of outreach to the local Ullama council, a religious group that advised the government on the conformity of government actions to Islam.

Koran Burning—Kabul, February 2012

Arriving back at MNBTK, the cultural clash between the population of Afghanistan and the ISAF forces erupted once again. The Taliban prisoners held at the Bagram prison were using their Korans to pass messages between themselves. These were confiscated by the guards, and without thinking, they implemented a normal procedure within the Western societies of destroying the material. Some Afghans working there either saw the Korans being burned or found the remnants of the burned Korans. The result was absolute chaos on the streets of Kabul as those opposed to our presence ramped up the media campaign of "infidels burn Koran" once again. All ISAF bases throughout Afghanistan instituted additional safety protocols, expecting the violent demonstrations to spread. MNBTK followed with canceling all outside-the-wire missions for twenty-four hours. There were sporadic shootings by Afghan police and military personnel turning on their ISAF mentors. Tragically, two US Army officers I had met at the Rule of Law Conference earlier in 2011 were shot and killed. They were mentors working inside the Ministry of Interior, and an ANP officer they worked with came up from behind them and shot them in the back of the head. We were all on edge given the number of Afghan guards we had around the base. Throughout the next ten months in Uruzgan, there were several incidents where Afghan soldiers turned on Australian soldiers. However, it would be a stretch to say they were all related to the Koran burning at the prison.

The general population of Uruzgan Province didn't seem to blink an eye over the event. News comes late to the remote province, but it seemed more than that. When we were again allowed to go outside the wire and meet with our judges and prosecutors, not one of them felt anything horrid had been done. Quite the contrary, MMJ was very vocal about how the Taliban burned hundreds of Korans every time they burned down a school, and nobody gets upset.

Touché, Shujai—The Hazaran Wild Card in Khas Uruzgan and the Conflict between the US-SOF Approach and That of US Conventional Forces

Uruzgan Province was originally the area occupied by the Dari-speaking Hazaran tribe of Afghanistan. Hence the name "Hazarangan," which was later "pasthunized" to Uruzgan as the Pashtu tribes started pushing them out. The Hazaran are Shia Muslims while the Pashtu are Sunni. The Hazaran are also oriental-looking due to the slaughter of all the males of the tribe in the early 1200s by the invader Genghis Khan. He replaced them with his own soldiers, giving rise to this racial separation that sits on top of all else. Uruzgan itself had been recently divided into two provinces, recognizing the strong Hazaran population in the northern mountains of Uruzgan. This new province was named Day Kundi and was unique in that the provincial governor was a female. The other area of Uruzgan heavily populated by Hazarans was the eastern part of Uruzgan known as Khas Uruzgan.

Khas Uruzgan is at a higher elevation than Tarin Kowt and very remote. The roads to the district were dangerous to travel since the Taliban was very active in the district. In the nearly three years I was there, it was not possible to get a prosecutor or judge out to the province because of safety concerns. The Hazaran, not being Pashtu, are vehemently opposed to the Taliban. Place that on top of the long-standing feud between them and the Pashtu that were constantly forcing them out of their own traditional tribal areas, and you have an explosive mix. When trying to establish governance, including criminal justice institutions, outsiders tend toward wanting to bring a proven system into an area where the institutions that were there before have seemingly collapsed rather than reestablishing the former and mentoring from there. I stand amazed at how historically there has been a complete naiveté when it comes to such things. The American Civil War was to be over in six weeks. Korea was to be a short police action, and not to mention the thoughts about our involvement in Vietnam. All historical lessons were totally left at the curb as we drove toward stability in rural Afghanistan.

Uruzgan was in such a quagmire—the traditional justice embraced by the area pushing back on the formal dynamic being pushed out by ISAF and the US embassy. UPRT's rule of law and justice efforts of working with the traditional as we mentored toward the formal creating a workable hybrid was an exception, not the rule. In the area of policing, all pretext of establishing a community police agency versus a paramilitary force to combat the Taliban had been abandoned by the US military. Reliance on the traditional tribal ways was the only viable, though imperfect, model. That said, when abuses occurred, there were charges and countercharges between the tribes and groups involved as each sought the favor of Kabul or ISAF for their positions.

In Khas Uruzgan, Abdul Hakim Shujai was a Hazaran strongman who had a running feud with the Pashtu strongman Ruy Mohammad. Both headed up Afghan Local Police (ALP) units in Khas Uruzgan. Though supposedly fashioned after the successful Sunni Awakening movement in Iraq, aka "Sons of Iraq," the ALP program struggled to be more than the traditional tribal vigilante program where local strongmen controlled given areas. Western thinkers had a real problem with the abuses and heralded that these ALP would constitute the next round of lawless bands of brigands after we left.

In Uruzgan, the commander of the Combined Team Uruzgan (CTU) in the summer of 2012 was a regular army colonel. He interacted with the provincial governor and MK, the provincial chief of police. Khas Uruzgan was Special Operations territory. The Village Stability Operations Program (VSOP) pursued by the US Army Green Berets and under the command at that time of the Navy SEAL commander "Mike." SEAL units were very kinetic—that is focused on engaging the enemy and removing them from the battlefield. However, VSOP came at the situation by enabling the local population to be self-sustaining, taking their "enemy" off the battlefield. As diverse as Khas Uruzgan was, they had several groups of ALP they worked with, trying to balance between the two tribal groups and stay neutral. This was imperative since they were not present in large numbers and had to rely on the locals for their own safety and support. The problem was their enemy often was the other local ALP commanders and their groups. Charges and countercharges of Taliban alliances and targeted killings under the guise of their official role as ALP abounded between the Hazaran Shujai and the Pashtu Ruy Mohammad. Claims of women being raped and innocents killed, the numbers often exaggerated or the event not even substantiated, were common. Shujai's claims that Ruy's group held many Taliban were just as credible as Ruy's claims that Shujai was carrying out unlawful killings. Both groups wanted the US forces to back them. Shujai was a proven ally of the US Special Forces operating in the area. The Hazaran were enemies of the Taliban Pashtu movement. MK, the new PCOP, was Pashtu, and he was trying to consolidate power in Khas Uruzgan.

In late July 2012, Shujai, responding to an alleged Taliban ambush that killed two of his men, attacked the Pashtu villages from which these alleged Taliban came from. The reports rang of Mongol raiders of the past centuries. Allegations of trashing, looting, and burning of houses were accompanied by allegations of the raping of women. Several men were taken hostage and later found dead. There was a huge uproar with the tribal fault lines straining at the seams all the way to Kabul. There were allegations that the US SOF was protecting Shujai. What played out revealed the strain between the SOF approach and that of our traditional army command at CTU. It also was a glaring example of the military command running full-steam ahead with "the solution" to the problem, in the process missing an opportunity to build the human infrastructure necessary to bring stability to a region with a history of conflict.

In the press, it was reported that the provincial chief of police, Matiullah Khan, travelled to Khas Uruzgan by helicopter to arrest both Ruy, who was also wanted for several murders in the area, and Shujai. Ruy was brought back, but Shujai avoided detainment. There were allegations that the SOF personnel in Khas Uruzgan tipped him off and helped him evade capture.[2] The truth would prove to be a little more ironically humorous with disastrous results.

The Afghan police don't have helicopters. PCOP Matiullah Khan couldn't safely travel to Khas Uruzgan because the Taliban-controlled sections of the road and others weren't cleared of IEDs. Therefore, he had to be taken by US forces. I have no knowledge of how the commander of the Combined Team Uruzgan came to bring MK by helicopter to Khas Uruzgan, but what unfolded at the meeting between the US colonel who commanded the CTU, MK, Ruy, Shujai, and a certain Green Beret on the ground there is revealing. This was a covert mission to arrest Ruy and Shujai. A meeting to discuss the issues with Ruy and Shujai was prearranged. The meeting seemed to focus on defusing the tensions between the Hazaran and Pashtu tribes in the area. As the meeting drew to a close, an invitation to return to Tarin Kowt aboard the helicopters was extended to both Ruy and Shujai, allegedly to continue the reconciliation talks. It was reported that discussions concerning armored vehicles and additional weapons were to be pursued once they got back to Tarin Kowt. My sources within the US-SOF confirmed that as the liftoff time for the helicopters approached, both Ruy and Shujai were expected to fly back to Tarin Kowt. What inducements were offered I couldn't say. I can say that as the helicopters were warming up, Shujai took a VSOP Green Beret aside and asked him if he must get on the helicopter. Shujai was not fooled for one moment that this was anything but a ruse to detain him. The Green Beret soldier told him he had no orders to put him on the helicopter and that the decision was his to make. As Ruy eagerly went aboard the helicopter, Shujai excused himself to use the latrine. He passed the latrine and kept right on walking until he was off the base. The CTU commander reportedly then exposed the whole thing for what it was, an elaborate ruse to detain both Ruy and Shujai. He began accusing the Green Beret of allowing a criminal to escape. This caused a cool feeling to fall between the CTU on Camp Holland and SOF on Camp Ripley that didn't leave until the CTU command was handed over to the Australians.

What struck me more than anything was the complete disregard shown for the Afghan legal system. The CTU command had long

---

[2] "Security at the Fringes: the case of Shurjai in Khas Uruzgan" by Martine Van Bijlert, April 6, 2013.

spoken of limiting MK's power. However, when given the opportunity to insert the courts and prosecutor's office between MK and his exercise of extra-judicial power, the CTU command failed to do so. The UPRT rule of law and justice advisors were certainly not consulted as to what our opinions were concerning this opportunity to mentor the Afghan police and prosecutors in handling such a high-profile case. Under Afghan law, not unlike many countries, the prosecutor conducts the investigation, and upon the prosecutor's request and evidence, the court issues an arrest warrant. It was a perfect opportunity to boost the image of the prosecutor's office in Uruzgan. The elders of Khas Uruzgan had been asking to bring a prosecutor and judge out to the district for quite some time. I'm not sure this line of procedure even entered the CTU commander's thoughts. There was just a total disconnect.

Shujai remained free, protected by his tribal and patronage system. Ruy was released, and the following year he became the deputy district police chief. However, in October 2012 a Pashtu working for the Khas Uruzgan police, in a command position, walked into the room at the district center where two VSOP Green Berets were standing. He was well known to them both. I too knew both of them, "Kash" and Ruiz. Kash spent time with me before heading out to Khas Uruzgan, discussing traditional justice and our efforts to tie the tribal elder groups back to the courts in Tarin Kowt while enjoying the night sky on the Taj Mah Deck. I was looking forward to him returning to Ripley to hear of his progress. However, that was not to be, for this trusted Pashtu ANP commander shot them both dead and then fled back into the arms of the Taliban.

I can't prove Shujai got it right when he claimed the Taliban came out of Ruy's ALP. What I do know is the failure to properly use the Afghan legal system, thereby putting all efforts to arrest both Ruy and Shujai on to the Afghans themselves, was a misplaced effort. It allowed allegations of the SOF-VSOP in Khas Uruzgan to be seemingly aligned with one group over the other. Did this lead to revenge killings on the part of the Pashtu? We will never know, but what if it was? Who paid the price? Certainly not the CTU commander.

The Camp Ripley Family: Jake "the Snake," "Mike," "Ed," "Tal," "Soda," "Mac," "Fast Eddie," "Kash," and "Dapper Dan"

Camp Ripley—the place where the DEFAC didn't open until 0730 because most of its inhabitants were operational well into the night—was the original US Marine Forward Operating Base (FOB) built in 2004 that housed the American PRT before the Netherlands forces took over operations in 2006. The Dutch built Camp Holland, leaving Ripley in the hands of the US-SOF command. Living on or even having access to Ripley, one got a vicarious sense of the high level of operations that came out of there. The camp had an energetic feel with few lights at night and special codes to enter the doors of the main operations center. Though I had clearance for most of the area, there were doors that were off limits, especially when the red light was circling outside of it. The tales I have are not those of killing but of the camp life of these SOF personnel. They were a mix of army, navy, and air force personnel who were more like a family within the larger context of their respective services. First names were commonly used between the ranks, but command lines were never crossed. Working out in their gym was not about weights and big muscle but of extreme cross-training, kettle bells, sledge pulls, and rope climbs with chains wrapped around your neck. Lean and endurance was the goal.

166

Very early on, I learned how different they were in their approach to interaction with the Afghans. While I saw almost a romantic desire by the US commanders of CTU conventional force to interact with MK long before he was provincial chief of police, the opposite was true with the SOF. MK wanted to be associated with them. It was a warrior-to-warrior relationship, each understanding the limits of the game. There was an ANA-SOF camp right next to Ripley, and they were mentored by both the US and Aussie SOF from Camps Ripley and Russell respectively. Both groups had a great attitude toward their mentees with a serious but jovial method that came across well in a culture where friendship mattered.

"Soda" was a tall air force officer heading up the VSOP who, working with Ted, our main State Department lead at the time, was instrumental in getting things cleared with the then SOF commander "Tal" to allow the State Department CHUs space and power hook-up on Ripley. Of course at the end of the day, Soda had his own CHU, a place to smoke his cigar in peace under the stars. His VSOP personnel had nice transit accommodations and taxi service to and from the air terminal at all hours of the day and night, provided by us at State. This arrangement lasted to the end. We at State enjoyed the extra company and duty.

"Eddie" came from alligator country where his family raised them. If I tell too many stories without first checking the statute of limitations concerning the transport of those creatures, I fear his detention by Texas law enforcement. Let's just say college frivolity, alcohol, and access to alligators combined to make absolutely hilarious, in hindsight, situations. Eddie, much younger than myself, came from the conservative South and held to such principles. This old, northern Midwestern liberal had ideas that clashed with his. However, we respected each other and talked through the differences. In the end, we weren't that far apart on the main principles the country should function on, just the road to follow to get there.

"Ed" was a big man with a big smile who worked human intelligence for the VSOP operations, tracking all the players. He and I would sit down after my missions into Tarin Kowt, and I would share with him my notes on meetings with the justice sector. He is also one lucky SOB. He lived in the one of the plywood hootches next to the Taj Mah Deck. One day he had taken in an early evening workout, and after coming back from his shower, he lay down in his bed instead of sitting up to Skype home, which was his norm at that time. The rocket that fell just outside his hootch sprayed shrapnel just above his body, peppering all the clothing he had on the opposite wall with holes. Life and death were just a fine line of luck we all grew to accept.

"Jake" would always make coffee runs down from Chora. He would prowl the tiny Camp Holland PX for any hint of coffee. I had reached out to my cousin from Oregon for whole-bean coffee and a hand grinder, given the on-again, off-again power situation when I first arrived. My cousin, once a naval lieutenant, came through with a rather large load given by the folks back home. Jake and the VSOP personnel up in Chora were in coffee hog heaven for quite some time.

Chora is the northern most of three major population centers in Uruzgan. It was in this region where the Bibi Aisha incident took place. Rumors and intelligence had it that the ANA in the area had reached an accord with the local Taliban elements not to engage them, in exchange for the Talib not to target them. Clearing the Taliban from Chora and elsewhere would fall to MK's ANP more than the Afghan Army. It was also the place where Dave, my Australian colleague, and Brad, the USMC captain, were nearly killed by a young suicide bomber. Jake and I would spend time on the deck discussing how to connect the courts and prosecutor's office in Tarin Kowt with Chora. Chora's judge at the time was an old mullah by the name of Dawd Mohammad. Dawd was the poster child for all the mullah jokes ever thought of and totally ineffective other than some symbolic indicator of the concept of an Afghan court system. The Dutch built a road between Tarin Kowt and Chora, finished in late 2011, at a cost of $32 million. I kept telling Jake to mentor the Afghans to send the criminal prisoners to TK via the road. He would laugh and say that some would think they were being sent that way because there was a high chance of getting killed. When the road was first proposed, many wanted it to be built through the desert area known as the "dash" that had been used as the preferred route for years. The Dutch decided to connect all the villages, following the river running between TK and Chora. After the road was finished, locals came back asking for another running through the dash. Seems there was a reason the population in Chora didn't want to go through all the villages along the river. It wasn't safe. A real judge wouldn't make it to Chora until early 2014, when MMJ would send the corrupt primary court chief judge's son-in-law, Judge Abdul Raziq, the former "muj" that could protect himself, along with a young prosecutor. This move was as much to break up the family corruption of the primary court as it was to get a judge up to Chora.

Judge Abdul Razeeq inside the primary court office

"Mac" operated out of the western regions of Uruzgan known as Shahid-e-Hasas. There was another town in the region named O'Shea for some long-ago errant Irishman who came to settle there. He had been in an out of there for nearly six years. He knew all the players. I can still see him and Jake dragging their gear off the Blackhawk late at night with tired smiles on their faces when they saw the white Toyota Hilux waiting to drive them and their gear back to Ripley. Sometimes, when they were coming in at zero dark thirty, they would contact us in advance, and we would just leave a truck for them with the key hidden in some designated location. Mac managed to make it through the whole six years rather unscathed, until the last weeks when he decided to go out on his own to take some final pictures on a four-wheel-drive gator. Fortunately, it was a small IED he triggered, but it was a close call. I just shook my head.

"Mike," the one SEAL team commander whom I got to know the best, stood tall even among such a select group. Extremely respected by the forces under his command, he ran an efficient, tight ship. He curtly put to rest the friction between the CTU and the SOF command over the Shujai arrest debacle, much to the appropriate hidden glee of those under his command that were close to the incident.

"Dan" had written a book about Uruzgan. If you didn't know that he had, he would remedy the situation with an autographed copy. As a member of the earliest US UPRT embedded with the US Marines on FOB Ripley, Dan had the benefit of having known who the Afghan players had been back in 2004, 2005, and 2006. Coming back with that knowledge in his role as an advisor to the SEAL team commander helped clarify many of the enigmas I was dealing with. The family ties of MK through his marriages were particularly important. Dan could go on for hours with the most mind-bending, sometimes seemingly irrelevant, irreverent, obtuse statements and questions that would engage and irritate at the same time. He often risked being thrown over the rail of the deck with some of his statements, but all in all, I found him most oddly engaging.

"Kash" was heading out to Khas Uruzgan and he stopped up to talk about how rule of law in such a tribal area would look a year from now. I gave him my accept them for what they have in the area of justice and mentor from there speech. He was keen to get to work and his bright smile pierced through his full beard. He looked the part and being a Muslim he was positioned to be very effective. I looked forward to seeing him back on the Taj Maj Deck soon.

A combined group of America's warrior SOF personnel walked around the State Deck CHU compound on a daily basis. Sitting out under the stars on the Taj Mah Deck, their conversations would float up to me. They were everyday conversations of home, family, and youthful activities. I often looked down from that perch, looking at their faces looking back at me. I saw reflected in them the faces of my USMC comrades back in Vietnam. I thought of the circle of life and the different roles we play throughout our own. I said a prayer for all of them each time the Osprey that took them from Ripley shook my CHU in the dark early hours of the morning.

Facing Reality: Recognizing the "Uruzgan Narco-State" as a Potential Contributing Source of Stability

Matiullah was a colonel in control of his own private Kandak (brigade) of private highway guards (KAU). The KAU controlled the road to Kandahar, and they guarded the convoys, which were the lifeblood of MNBTK. It had been reported that he had been earning $2.5 million every month for that protective service. Many called him a warlord, but he was a new breed of warlord/strongman who also wanted official government recognition. This was the road that Indian and Pakistani warlords had taken in the past. MK was the wealthiest man in Uruzgan. His wealth came from many sources. I knew the legal ones, his government position and convoy protection, and assumed there was also the illegal. To think otherwise would be naïve. His convoy protection was a perfect conduit for moving opium out of Uruzgan. I knew he moved people because we once received two Toyota Hilux pickup trucks from Kandahar that were moved in his convoy. The containers that held the trucks, supposedly under seal, as they traveled on a large flatbed trailer arrived full of human feces and soaked with urine from the human contraband that also traveled inside the container. The Taliban knew he was their direct competition, and he was the one person who could extend security in the province. Opium is a major source of income for the Taliban, and cornering the market on the opium was a way to starve the Taliban and feed the rest of Uruzgan. That was certainly something MK wouldn't allow to slip past his notice. However, in early 2011, MK, with all his money and power, was not the chief of police in the province. He didn't have the authority to extend his protection beyond the highways. However, he did extend his power through his own ishula/*eslihi* peace and reform shura, and his KAU protected and enforced its rulings.

Opium is the main currency of the region, and though MMJ was against the use of it, he understood the role it played in bringing cash to the region. MMJ and I talked in terms of using that income to construct a functioning civil society in Uruzgan. Would this be a deal with the devil? Maybe, but opium was at their doorstep, not donor cash tied up or syphoned off in Kabul. Kabul's inability or unwillingness to fund Uruzgan properly gave them little choice. We never spoke about who was or wasn't involved in drug trade. MMJ opposed opium on a moral basis because the damage it was doing to Afghans who used it. However, sale and export of the product was a different story, especially if it could be done legitimately. The sad reality the world around, where the state fails to deliver the environment where farming or manufacturing of some sort can flourish, is that a culture of crime emerges with drugs and human trafficking leading the way. MMJ often preached about the evil of pedophilia that was very common in the region. We discussed the many aspects of how drugs were grown around the world and how India, Australia, and South Africa grew opium poppies in a controlled environment, allowing a legitimate trade to prosper. I was often amazed at his knowledge of the subject.

Uruzgan is a place where most people were focused on eating tomorrow, and therefore food security was paramount. Attacking the opium trade threatened that, and efforts toward eradicating opium would bring instability far quicker than the Taliban. Follow this example and ask yourself what choice did the farmer have in all this? The Uruzgan farmer, like all others around the world, needs cash for financing his legal crops. He would need to take out a loan, just as a farmer in Iowa would. The problem is there is only one bank in town, and it didn't give out farm loans. The bank struggled to provide even basic services, such as money transfers. The farmer is forced to get a loan from powerful people, and if those people don't have an interest in that family, then the farmer is forced to go to those connected to smuggling, human trafficking, the drug trade, as well as the Taliban. His collateral was that portion of his crop he set aside for poppy growth. When the government came through and destroyed his poppy plants, he would be forced to sell a daughter or son into slavery to pay off the debt. That slavery was at best sexual in nature, at worst a new suicide bomber. Now ask this question: what action would locals, who held government positions that enforced the laws of the nation, were targets of the Taliban, and wanted the best for their people, take against poppy grown in the region? I often used the phrase, "You're not from around here, are you, boy?" when trying to convey the sense of Uruzganis knowing they had to find their own way through this mess if they were going to not only survive but prosper. Afghanistan had become an opium nation long before we came. It was the reality of the region; for better or worse, it was the base of the economy. Absent a mass eradication effort, which would necessitate a massive international funding effort to provide food and alternate crop production, it was here to stay for the foreseeable future. So given it was staying, what options were open to mentor toward?

Legalization was one such option. However, all such conversation concerning that option fell on not just deaf but hostile ears. The International Narcotics and Law Enforcement (INL), a division of the US Department of State, was unwilling or unable to embrace opium's legitimate production and processing as a means to create jobs and bolster the economy of the region. Therefore, using the illegal but plentiful opium for the good of the community versus allowing it to destroy the community was the key. Stability in the region depended on controlling the opium trade for the good of Uruzgan, which demanded all the justice sector actors to reach an understanding of what would be prosecuted and what would not.

Let me explain here INL's position and mandate that conflicted with mine, even though we were both working for the US Department of State. My mandate was to create a stable environment where a criminal justice system could flourish. INL's mandate was to eradicate the production of poppy. They clashed head-on into the policy held by the Afghan government that aerial spreading to eradicate the poppy fields was forbidden and the US policy that recognized that eradicating a farmer's main cash crop would drive them into the Taliban camp. I approached INL with studies that showed there was a worldwide shortage of opium for conversion into pain medications. I also produced the Report of the Global Commission on Drug Policy, whose commissioners included George Shultz, Kofi Annan, and Richard Branson, and Paul Volker's recently published report showing the utter failure of the effort known as "the war on drugs." The report stated the following:

> The global war on drugs has failed, with devastating consequences for individuals and societies around the world. Fifty years after the initiation of the U.N. Single Convention on Narcotic Drugs, and 40 years after President Nixon launched the U.S. government's war on drugs, fundamental reforms in national and global drug control policies are urgently needed. Vast expenditures on criminalization and repressive measures directed at producers, traffickers and consumers of illegal drugs have clearly failed to effectively curtail supply or consumption.

It went on to recommend that world governments "experiment with models of legal regulation of drugs to undermine the power of organized crime and safeguard the health and security of their citizens."[3]

I pointed out to the INL representative in Kandahar that India, South Africa, and Australia had legal poppy growers where the product was controlled, refined, and transferred to pharmaceutical companies for use in the production of pain medication. These countries have had a long-term relationship with Afghanistan. I argued we should put the main cash crop of Afghanistan onto a similar path. This conversation became a bit heated because I wasn't a law enforcement officer. When I pointed out that I had graduated with honors with a BS in criminal justice and worked as a criminal lawyer for years, it was unpersuasive. I then gave him a quote from my organized crime and narcotics instructor from 1975 at the University of Toledo: "Most drugs will remain illegal because there is too much money in keeping them so." This prompted several e-mail exchanges where I was educated on the ins and outs of the opium trade, which ended with the obvious observation that if the refining process isn't performed well, then a large percentage of the product will end up in the illegal market. I replied, "So you are saying having 100 percent going into the illegal trade is preferable to say 50 to 80 percent, correct?" I never received a response. It was clear that taking the most profitable crop in the area and turning its production into a legitimate enterprise was of no interest to anyone. I guess my old university instructor was correct. Now the only question would be who would control the production and to what ends. In the summer of 2012, I chose the people of Uruzgan.

What Was Governance in 2012 Uruzgan? Who Controlled It?

We had a democratic petri dish of multiple tribal elder groups in our hands. From on high, there was a demand of an acceptance of twenty-first-century Western democracy systems and ideas rather than developing what already existed into an "Afghan acceptable democratic system" that had the potential to bring stability quickly. Governors coming from outside Uruzgan were seen as coming to line their pockets with Uruzgan's wealth. The new PGOV, Amir Achundzada, who arrived in

---

3. "War on Drugs: Report of the Global Commission on Drug Policy," June 2011.

April 2012, would be no exception. No government can operate without a solid economic base, and opium was the base in Uruzgan. Matiullah Khan, strongman, drug lord, and provincial chief of police, sat on top of it all, and he and the new PGOV eyed each other cautiously across the table upon which it rested. The chief judge MMJ had been reaching out to all the elders of the province as well as MK. MK was going to need additional community support to stand up to the new PGOV, who came from a powerful family from Helmand that was also linked to the opium trade. I saw MMJ as the key to bringing enough of the traditional justice system together with the formal justice system to create a justice shura that had enough influence to bring about change in the province.

Make no mistake about it—the justice sector is a governing body, especially where the lives of the people living there are one of day-to-day survival. How justice is administered affects the daily lives of Uruzganis more than what projects the provincial government brings to the area. Justice systems that the people accept are directly tied to the stability of an area. In communities around the world where the justice sector is seen as working for the people, there is stability. Where it is seen as a source of oppression, there is civil unrest or conflict. Government is only stable with the consent of the governed. MK didn't have that consent, and an alliance with MMJ would hold the key to solidifying his legitimacy to hold the power in Uruzgan. The necessary forces to bring these two together for their own benefit and the common good of the people of Uruzgan were in place.

However, in the spring of 2012, I couldn't do anything more than speak to MMJ because MK was still, from the ISAF side, the exclusive property of the military mentors. I was fortunate in that a new police-mentoring unit had come in December 2011. Col. Gilliam was the unit commander, and he was very open to me attending his team's meetings with MK. I took advantage of that generous offer, given the MRAPs his unit was using had very limited seating. This allowed me to push MK to attend the upcoming legal shura to be held at the provincial courthouse.

The Uruzgan AIHRC director, Dr. Stanikzai, was also urging MK's attendance. Dr. Stanikzai had taken the approach with MK that he could accomplish more advances in human rights in the region by focusing on rewarding MK for his positive behavior concerning his ANP than hammering on the negative. That was about to pay off. Though MK didn't attend the next legal shura, when all the members wanted to report him to the ministry of interior and demand that he come, MMJ and Dr. Stanikzai consoled against confronting MK using outside force. Instead they urged that the next legal shura should be held at the new provincial police headquarters. They would just "drop in" for a visit, thus triggering the Afghan-required hospitality toward travelers who arrive unannounced at your home. The group agreed, though in this case it wouldn't be totally unannounced, to allow MK to prepare to host the event, but he had no real choice; they were coming. It was like lighting a torch to kerosene on top of the one of the surrounding mountains.

Police Headquarters Becomes the Center of Government

The next six months would see a complete reversal of the first six frustrating months of my time in Uruzgan. The US government, through the army corps of engineers, had constructed a rather large ANP headquarters compound on the northeast side of town. It looked like the fort it was meant to be—guard towers along the walls, on all the corners, and flanking the entrance with its large steel gate covering several acres of land. Contained within the walls were multiple buildings with barracks housing for the ANP soldiers, not officers, as well as a logistics warehouses and office complexes.

Scotty inside the new PPHQ

It was the crown jewel of the many compounds MK controlled. Increasing his status exponentially, this compound became the Mecca for tribal people seeking resolution of issues at the feet of MK. The PGOV's compound paled in comparison. This sprawling modern facility was a model of waste and unsustainability. It followed in the footsteps of the modern prison built by the Dutch across town that became nothing more than a concrete warehouse overcrowded with humanity that shivered in the winter and suffered the heat in the summer. The generator power needed to run the electrical needs was huge, and the fuel needed to run those generators would cost far beyond what the Afghan government was willing to send to Uruzgan. So there was no heat in the winter and no air-conditioning in the stifling heat of summer.

The author inside the new Uruzgan provincial police
HQ compound

However, the PHQ, unlike the prison, was in the hands of MK, and he had sources of income outside of the government. Only time will tell how well this elephant will perform. It was certainly a far cry from the HESCO-reinforced walls of the old headquarters in the center of town. Over the next six months, I would lobby hard for the courts to take over the old provincial police headquarters so they could create a justice center, placing the prosecutor and all the court's offices within a central compound, allowing a more efficient interaction between their offices. It would also free up the homes the Dutch built for the judges and their families to be used for that purpose.

The author at the old ANP provincial HQ

That would assist in getting quality judges to the area. That would not happen, but at least a new police reaction unit would occupy it, and the courthouses that sat just outside the walls of the old headquarters would be well protected.

PGOV Achundzada Misses the Opportunity

"All I want you to do is brief the new governor on the status of the rule of law efforts in Uruzgan," Tim stated to me in frustration. Tim had replaced Ted as the main US State Department person on UPRT back in July 2011 and was approaching his one-year rotation back to Washington, DC. Ted had disengaged from the Australian-led and dominated PRT because, as the most senior civilian on the US part of the team, he resented the politics that put a junior Australian at the helm of director, over him, when the Australian director was absent from the PRT. Tim, on the other hand, had managed to make a fresh start with the new UPRT director and fell right into a very good working relationship with the Australians by heading up the governance mentoring efforts. Amir Achundzada had been at the post of Uruzgan's PGOV only a few months, and Tim wanted me to keep my presentation short and to the point while I, on the other hand, saw it as an opportunity to challenge the new PGOV to get involved where the other PGOVs had not. Lack of support from the office in the past had created problems for the courts and prosecutors. Also, a power struggle between his office and MK was coming, and as much as I thought MK was the main hope for Uruzgan in the short run, it would be preferable for the PGOV to take the lead in helping the justice sector come together in the province. I wanted to lay out for the PGOV the past disconnect between the justice sector and his office in addition to bringing him up to speed as to how the legal shura was starting to coalesce into a major governance entity that could be leveraged to bring stability to the province.

Like many persons at the US Department of State Foreign Service, Tim was a son of missionaries. Tim and his brother grew up in Pakistan, and his macro knowledge of the region was beyond question. However, I felt strongly that the subtle micro politics of Uruzgan that could help stabilize the province were not being fully exploited, and I wanted to push the new PGOV to engage the legal shura or at least have a conversation concerning its value to the region.

Malavi Mohammad Jan and General Zafar on a trip to Khas Uruzgan
with the new PGOV, Amir Achundzada (not shown), April 2012

Achundzada knew the value of MMJ as a religious figure even if he didn't seem to value his position as the chief judge of Uruzgan. He took MMJ with him on his whirlwind tour of the province early on. It was all a show on Achundzada's part because MMJ gave him credibility, but he certainly wasn't giving anything in return by supporting the justice sector needs. The new PGOV had sent no representatives to the two legal shuras held since he had arrived. Tim understood my passion but insisted on "just a briefing" the PGOV.

Amir Achundzada had rapidly gained a reputation at UPRT as being an arrogant, prideful person. My first meeting with him did nothing to diminish that image. Our PRT director, Adrian, and Tim were both discussing issues with Amir concerning the nearly completed, large, and very expensive government shura building that was soon to open on the compound. Despite those issues, it seemed that all Amir, who hadn't been in Uruzgan more than a half-dozen weeks or so, could do was complain about our unwillingness to replace the modest deputy governor's building, which had been severely damaged during the attack back in July 2011, with a new, large million-dollar complex. Never mind the DPGOV had an office in the large provincial government office building, which seemed to be struggling with the completion of its interior electrical, plumbing, and fitting out with furniture, Amir was pushing for a contract that he could farm out to increase his patronage power. However, no other big projects were in the pipeline for this governor. The last big one, the provincial police HQ, would be turned over to his rival in late May.

Overlooking damaged DPGOV building from new
provincial government shura building

DPGOV building after July 2011 attacks

New provincial government office building
under construction, December 2010

When it came time for me to brief Amir, Tim barely had my name out before the PGOV started to tell me about "his" legal shura and the good relationship he had with its members. Knowing the contrary to be true, I just responded with the fact that I worked closely with the provincial chief judge MMJ. That since I had been in the province since December 2010, I had worked with four chief prosecutors, three police chiefs, and he was now the second PGOV. I punctuated that with putting to him the question, "What do you wish to know from me about the justice situation here?" With a wave of his hand, he brushed the question aside and again began talking about how *his* legal shura had the situation well under control. I asked him when *his* legal shura would next meet. He replied that they met every month and that I should come to the next shura. I told him that I would look forward to his invitation. The invitation never came. Amir Achundzada had just let a foundation for controlling Uruzgan slip through his fingers into the hands of his rival. Over the next seven months, the justice sector actors would be hosted by the new provincial chief of police, BG Matiullah Khan, as he extended his power through embracing the legal shura that Malavi Mohammad Jan thought "was a good thing" to keep going back in 2011 but that neither the PCOP's office at that time nor any PGOV would embrace. Through MMJ, the move would bring tribal leaders once opposed to MK to accept that he, for now, was a new elder of Uruzgan and not just an illiterate warlord out for his own interest. In the summer of 2014, charges that Achundzada had illegally skimmed money from projects in Uruzgan would bring protests in the streets of Tarin Kowt with demands for his prosecution.[4]

Summer 2012: Training in High Gear and the Emergence of an Afghan Hero

The fighting season was upon us. There would be more casualties that impacted not only us but upon my Afghan counterparts. I was heavily focused on several training programs for the justice sector that were finally making their way to Tarin Kowt. Though planned many months ago, the combination of weather, personnel, and security issues had delayed them. The simple truth was one had to be committed to years of effort to get training programs out to the more remote regions of Afghanistan. Much was lost by the six to twelve-month deployment commitments of most personnel. It just wasn't enough time to work all the necessary logistics needed to bring things together, and the start and stop generated by such short rotations killed many efforts because one person's passion didn't necessarily follow the person he or she replaced.

Shane from TF-66 had chased down, literally, EUPOL to bring down a program geared to develop coordinated efforts between the police and the prosecutor's office. Fittingly it was labeled with the acronym of CoPP, which stood for Cooperation of Police and Prosecutor program. He had flown to Kabul looking for a program to help TF-66 in their mentoring efforts between the ANP quick reaction force (QRF) and the prosecutors under Col. Hanif, the political crimes prosecutor. Going from embassy to embassy, compound to compound, Shane hammered on any door he could find. He arrived at the EUPOL compound, and they had just the program. It would come in several modules. It would also be a huge success by bringing the police and the other justice sector actors closer in the field. It was an important first

---

[4.] *Sydney Morning Herald*, Rory Callinan, February 10, 2014.

step that showed MK a bigger picture of what it meant to be the PCOP and thus part of a systematic approach to criminal justice.

Col. Hanif, who lived in Uruzgan, embraced the program fully while the new chief civil prosecutor, Abdul Hadi Hamkar, would do so reluctantly. He wished to start a program of his own that he would teach. Relationships between that office and the police were strained due to the corruption of the previous chief civil prosecutor, a man by the name of Mustafa. Mustafa was also from outside Uruzgan and fit the bill of a person who came to Uruzgan to steal from it. He ran into opposition by the judges, and within two months he was gone. I put him on an Embassy Air flight back to Kabul. He was complaining bitterly about the backward people in Uruzgan who couldn't be trusted. Knowing his backstory from MMJ, I just looked at him and facetiously said, "Well, I guess I'm sending off the last honest man in Uruzgan." He just glared at me and said good-bye.

Mustafa

Hamkar's arrival was welcomed by some of the assistant prosecutors but not all. Mustafa had brought some of the assistant prosecutors with him. Unfortunately, what they were promised by him and the attorney general's office compared to what was delivered were two different things. The AGO was very corrupt. Most of the assistant prosecutors that came down were filling patronage jobs. They hounded UPRT to supplement their salaries and provide transport to and from

Kabul constantly. We refused on all occasions, referring them back to the AGO and the funding it was receiving from the international community from the top. The AGO would say to them that they must not have a good relationship with the PRT. This was the prime example of the duel government created earlier by the PRT system that we were trying to break. Most of Mustafa's protégés quit when he left, leading to a complete shakeup of the Uruzgan civil prosecutor's office, which hobbled its efforts.

In contrast, Hamkar was a straightforward prosecutor who brought professionalism to the local civil prosecutor's office. He had strong anticorruption credentials from Zabul before he came to Uruzgan. Arriving in March 2012, I learned that Mustafa had been more focused on his team reading Islamic materials and focusing on their faith instead of their work. Hamkar, it was joked, was moved from Zabul not to bring corruption under control in Uruzgan but to prevent him from doing so in Zabul. The irony of it all was that Mustafa was then sent to Zabul.

Hamkar had survived an assassination attempt by two Talib in Kandahar a few years before. They had him and his son on their knees with a gun to the side of his head. Moving just as the trigger was pulled, Hamkar, suffering a bullet through his cheek and out through his jaw, disarmed his assailant, killed him, and wounded the other. He sported a heavy beard, and he would say the length was determined by how close the Taliban threat was. He was a personable man who wrote poetry and would always insist we couldn't leave his office until he recited his latest masterpiece. His beard was as thick as the fancy lambskin hat that adored his head, a sign of his stature, since they were quite expensive. I found him to be a sincere man who was proud of his family, which consisted of two sons and a daughter from his one and only wife of forty years. He often spoke of her in the dearest of terms. He was a proud man, and because of that, Hamkar would make a critical error. He started to look into corruption at the primary court. Rather than working through the local group or legal shura, he took his findings to Kabul. That caused a strong backlash against him. He would later apologize, but it did not sit well with the group dynamics.

Right to left: LTC Johnston of the US JAG, Hamkar, Mirwis
Ghani, the author, Salihi, unknown, and unknown

The other thing that hurt Hamkar was his view, correct under the law, that the police should come to him and take orders from him as it concerned the investigation of civil crimes. It was obvious he felt MK was beneath him, that the province was backward, and that he knew best. Though he would go and talk with Col. Ghulab, the well-educated, Western-dressed, former communist, chief ANP investigator who kept a bottle of scotch in his desk drawer, he just wouldn't work with MK.

The civil prosecutor's office would make great strides under Hamkar, and he would work together with the Australian Federal Police and US police mentors working at the ANP training center on MNBTK, teaching the role of the civil prosecutor in pursuing everyday crime that was not concerned with acts against the state, such as terrorism, which was Col. Hanif's role.

True to form, the EUPOL CoPP program wouldn't get fully implemented in Uruzgan until the man responsible for bringing it, Shane from TF-66, had left. He had, however, passed it on to UPRT and our rule of law and justice group with such enthusiasm that we had adopted it during that critical stage between Shane leaving and his replacement, Trent, coming on. Trent had an attraction to explosives and would often go chasing down an opium refining facility along with the Afghan QRF. Once found, they would always blow up the crude refining facility. Trent would set the explosives. Once he related to me how he had packed a few gas cooking containers alongside his charges and then, while in the process of completing his other tasks, had forgotten about the cooking containers. That is, until he detonated the charge, sending them shooting into the sky as errant missiles. I just shook my head and laughed at his escapades—until he managed to tangle with an IED. Injured but recovering well, he handed the CoPP program off to the UPRT once again. Truth is we were glad to have it, and it showed how well the integration of the several command efforts had become by June 2012.

The instructors that came down with the CoPP program were high-ranking ANP investigators from Kabul. These highly educated and experienced investigators were well received by both the prosecutor and police from Uruzgan. They really hit it off, and though we had them set up at a hotel that catered to contractors on MNBTK, they would head off to Tarin Kowt to socialize with Col. Hanif after class.

The logistics of having the program for a full week were exhausting, and again the groups pulled together to make it all run smoothly. MNBTK had two rings of walls. The Afghans guarded the outer wall while Slovakian guards guarded an inner wall that surrounded Camp Holland. Aussie SF and US Army soldiers guarded Camp Russell and Camp Cole respectively. Camp Ripley had mostly an Afghan private security firm handling their interior security, supplemented by soldiers and seaman from the US-SOF. This arrangement would be cited by the US embassy for pulling all US diplomatic personnel eight months early from UPRT in the spring of 2013 after a tragedy occurred in Zabul Province.

That tragedy occurred while the State Department was delivering one of the first loads of schoolbooks under a program called "My Afghan Library." I heard several accounts of what happened with accusations of incompetence and finger pointing. However, Monday-morning quarterbacking serves no useful purpose and diminishes the wonderful people who placed their lives at risk throughout Afghanistan. What is clear is a large vehicle-borne IED took the lives of US diplomat Ann Smedlinghoff and three US service personnel, and the personal interpreter for the senior civilian representative for RC South, Ambassador Jonathan Addleton, escaped injury or death by pure luck. Another female State Department civilian was placed in a vegetative state. The US embassy did a knee-jerk reaction, and what followed resulted in the Regional Security Office finding fault in almost every outstation, justifying the rapid pullout of all civilian staff. The US embassy declared that the security provisions at MNBTK were insufficient, as it had Afghan security on the outer walls. Given the loaming sequester and the pressure to downsize at the Department of State, the outcome was sadly very predictable. It would lead to a feeling of abandonment on the part of the civilian Australian UPRT contingent, and rightfully so.

However, that incident was several months away. Arranging through the Joint Command Center to use a building used by the Afghan Army, the Australian Federal Police provided the chairs every morning while my Aussie colleague David and I provided transportation of the Afghan personnel attending the CoPP program from the front gate to the training location. Additionally, we delivered morning snacks, tea, and lunch, which I arranged through the cook who serviced the Afghan private security guards that guarded the outer wall. David and I, drenched in sweat from the summer heat and dust, carrying hot pots of lamb, rice, and flatbread, were quite a sight. The program was very successful with the classes that summer, including the trial of two murder cases in Tarin Kowt at the provincial court of appeals resulting in convictions. PGOV Achundzada actually showed up for the closing ceremony and handed out the diplomas.

Col. Hanif speaking to the CoPP attendees at graduation

PGOV Amir Akandzada delivering the certificates of completion
and criminal statutes of Afghanistan to CoPP attendees

In addition to the CoPP program, we brought in additional JSSP training in the area of human rights, which was attended by females, a huge step in Uruzgan. Their presence was no accident, for Dr. Stanikzai of the AHIRC was very active behind the scenes in Tarin Kowt.

Dr. Stanikzai began pushing and pulling all the justice sector actors toward better cooperation. It was nothing short of a heroic effort. He alone organized two legal shuras without our presence or involvement. He went from MK's office to MMJ's courthouse with regularity, stopping by Col Hanif and Hamkar's office regularly.

Dr. Stanikzai and I would often speak about how to involve the justice sector in solving human rights violations rather than just reporting them to Kabul. Human rights and a functioning criminal justice system go hand in hand. The value of encouraging Matiullah Khan to bring disciplinary action or prosecution of his police officers accused of human rights abuses would bear fruit. He did start doing just that, not in all cases, but enough so that his actions were also taken as a measure of the status of human rights and not just the raw statistics documenting human rights violations. MK began to get his feet under him in his position as PCOP, and his positive actions gained him respect in some circles from Kabul. This respect opened the doors for Dr. Stanikzai to continue influencing MK to work with MMJ. He was so successful that in October 2012 the head of the AIHRC would come to Tarin Kowt and attend the legal shura to praise all of them for their efforts. This included praise for the formation of a women's shelter protected by MK and operated by the Directorate of Women Afghanistan (DOWA), not an NGO, which was the norm throughout Afghanistan. That accomplishment was earth-shattering in a place where in the fall of 2010 they ran midwife program workers out of Tarin Kowt at gunpoint. I received calls of misbelief from colleagues in Kabul because nowhere had the locals, without an NGO, set up such a shelter. The cultural perception was that such places were actually houses of prostitution and were targets of attacks. However, this shelter was under MK's protection, and since locals ran it, such accusations didn't emerge.

The next legal shura was set for September at the new provincial police headquarters. Things were accelerating, and Dr. Stanikzai would begin receiving even more threats against his life. He was obviously in fear. He began approaching me to write a letter to the US embassy with hopes of qualifying for a visa program aimed at helping Afghans who worked for the United States to immigrate. However, he didn't slow down his efforts.

August was waning, and the first legal shura to be held at the new PHQ was just three weeks away. Dr. Stanikzai wanted to meet before the day arrived, so we brought him onto Camp Holland to have relaxed conversation and enjoy a cafe latte. Greeting him at the front gate with its usual hustle and bustle was a little nerve-racking since in addition to our usual Afghan private security guards, who we knew, there were several Afghan National Army personnel at the gate. MMJ's earlier warning about being careful around these people from outside Uruzgan would constantly ring in my ear.

Dr. Stanikzai arrived with his usual warm smile, and we greeted each other warmly. He was fairly fluent in English, so there was no need for an interpreter. We engaged in small talk through the multiple layers of security checkpoints required to get an Afghan onto Camp Holland. Finally we arrived at the Green Bean coffee stand that sat just outside of Poppies. With its Starbucks-like setup, it was always a popular spot. It had opened about ten months earlier as one of the examples of schizophrenic projects for troop comforts in a place that was supposed to be winding down. It was over his latte that Dr. Stanikzai began to tell the tales of the undercurrents flowing within the Uruzgan power structure.

In late June, PGOV Achundzada brought MMJ to Kabul with him in an attempt to meet with all the ministers to discuss the lack of funding through those ministries as well as tribal issues, mainly the Popalzai first agenda that was being pursued. The ministers didn't treat them well, so MMJ called on President Karzai. Karzai called a meeting of his ministers, and it was there that MMJ talked of the simple people of Uruzgan. People overlooked by Kabul as undeserving, illiterate, and not worthy of their efforts. He directly spoke to the minister of interior, telling him if he couldn't handle the Taliban in the area, then let the people of Uruzgan deal with them. He told him, "Our families are ready to join the police." He went on to chastise the minister of education for the corruption within his ministry in Uruzgan, which was stealing education from the children. MOE claimed 180,00 students when the PGOV showed only 1,800 and 170 schools when the PGOV showed only seventy. MMJ stated that the minister didn't know the reality within Uruzgan. MMJ told me that President Karzai told his ministers that, "He was shamed by their inattention to Uruzgan and its people." MMJ went on to say that the "mud in the water of Uruzgan came from the spring." It is an old Afghan saying referring to the source of the problem, and he was laying it at their feet. Before the meeting was over, MMJ and PGOV Achundzada were promised three million dollars for their Uruzgan district government issues. It was an eye opener for Achundzada of MMJ's reach into the seat of power in Kabul.

It was during this time that there were indicators of MMJ waffling between the PGOV and MK, but he told me that he was constantly working the issues between all with power for the best of Uruzgan. Also, Col. Hanif and Mohammad Zai, the internal affairs prosecutor, were investigating Hamkar. Mustafa, trying to get his job back, had accused him of un-Islamic behavior consisting of failure to pray and fast. Much of that may have been triggered by Hamkar's taking his grievances concerning the primary court chief judge Haji Abdul Wahid and Mustafa seeing an opening to press his way back in.

Dr. Stanikzai had taken the initiative with Hamkar and Col. Gulab, the chief police investigator, to build on the CoPP training and work directly with the two of them to move cases forward. Coupled with that were the rather impressive statistics coming out of the court showing a huge increase in the caseload moving through the system. Over one thousand cases, a far cry from the sixty for 2010, had cleared the courts over the last Afghan year.

MK had moved his command into the new PHQ in July and had ordered Omar Khan, the strong Deh Rawud police chief, to Chora, an obvious power play on MK's part. That order would stand ignored until a deal was struck bringing Omar into MK's inner circle. In the meantime, Dr. Stanikzai was bringing allegations of police torture to MK, who seemed to embrace the process, using his internal affairs prosecutor Mohammad Zai but with the caveat of keeping the investigation local. That included any punishment issues. This would be a mentoring point both the AIHC and I would focus on with MK.

With all the headway Dr. Stanikzai was making, I sat my coffee down and looked at him with a smile. I told him he had become my Afghan hero. He looked at me with an inquisitive look as I took him back in time to our conversations concerning the nexus between a functioning criminal justice system and human rights. He had found that sweet spot among all the actors, helping them to see the greater picture, their shared common interest. This was not just a professional interest but also one of physical survival. Without the population of Uruzgan wanting them protected, they would be easy targets of the Talib once the ISAF forces were gone. Having a criminal justice system that served the people was essential to their survival. What had been accomplished over the summer was done only because he carried the message and pushed and pulled the members of the legal shura to work together every day. He was the behind-the-scenes energy that made it all happen.

The Seismic Shift

Arriving at the new provincial police compound for the first legal shura to have the provincial chief of police, along with his command officers and internal affairs prosecutor, in attendance was a huge milestone. Gone were the days where prosecutors and judges were not adequately protected and without proper transportation. The US police mentor commander, Col. Gilliam, had provided transport for my interpreter and me. It was also the first time the US military person who worked directly with MK would be attendance. It was to be a seismic shift in how the justice sector in Uruzgan interacted.

Dismounting the MRAP, I removed my personal protection equipment (PPE), storing it on my seat. The new provincial police HQ compound was a large, open area where ANP manned the guard towers, looking down on the area, while others walked the area going to and from their duties. Given the uptick in Afghan police turning on ISAF personnel, I knew that the Diplomatic Security Department would not approve. I won't say I didn't feel exposed, but it was one of those moments that the message I sent by my behavior had to be "I feel safe here."

Walking up to the building where the shura was to be held, it was obvious MK was setting the stage for the future. Flanking the walkway up to the door of the new air-conditioned and solar-powered building were two Afghan national flags. I paused as I pictured the old provincial courthouse that had been the venue in the past. I thought, *Well, here we go.* Stepping through the door, the halls were full of ANP scurrying about. As we climbed up the stairs to the second floor, I ran into the Huquq director, Abdul Mohammad, whose phone with the chirping bird ring tone began its song. He just looked at me and laughed as I began to mimic it while looking around for the bird making the sounds. Rounding the corner, LTC Hotaki, the counter-narcotics chief, was sitting on a chair inside the room. When he saw me, he rose, and we embraced. Hotaki had attended every one of the JSSP classes we brought into Tarin Kowt. I would tease him about which counter he put the opium under.

MK's meeting facility on the new PPHQ compound

Those moments of humorously stating the obvious allowed us to focus on the things that were important to the people. I would see him a few weeks later coming out of the limited-access intelligence building inside the Camp Holland command compound. He was with two apparently new "spooks" on the base, for I didn't recognize them, and they stood in complete shock as he, in his Afghan garb, and I gleefully embraced each other as they were walking by. It was one of those moments when I knew I had been in Uruzgan far longer than most on MNBTK.

Looking around the room, I could see Hamkar, the civil chief prosecutor, and two of his assistants. His beard was rather short compared to its length when he first came. The thought crossed my mind that he must have felt safer from the Taliban now. Crossing the room toward him, he smiled, and, embracing, we exchanged greetings. He knew he was going to have to deal with his breach of the local cultural protocol, the "keep it local" rule, concerning the primary court chief judge, Haji Abdul Wahid's, actions. However, all and all, he was doing well.

Turning around, I caught the police internal affairs prosecutor, Mohammad Zai, coming through the door. He now had his office on the first floor of this building. He told me MK and he met on a regular basis to discuss ANP misconduct. Though he admitted that getting MK to take action against certain checkpoint commanders was proving difficult. Col. Hanif from the political crimes/terrorism prosecutor's office entered along with two of his assistants that I knew. Dr. Stanikzai followed him closely through the door, along with Haji Abdul Wahid and his son-in-law Abdul Raeeq, but still no MMJ.

The room was filling up, and I was surprised to see Rana, the director of Women's Affairs (DOWA) in attendance. This was truly a first on many levels. I was beginning to think MMJ wasn't going to make it. He wasn't always at the shuras held back in his courthouse, but I couldn't image he would not be here unless the PGOV had pulled an internal coup, which wasn't likely. Then I looked out the window and saw MMJ's armored SUV pull up to take its place in front of the building. I watched as his sons put their PST training to good use.

When MMJ entered the room, all rose, and the bowing accompanied by the hand kissing ritual began. It took several minutes. I always stayed back and waited for the ritual to run its course before making myself known. Once our eyes met, we came toward each other, embracing in our usual Afghan manner. When I pulled back from him, I just smiled and asked, "So MK has passed a test toward being more than just a man with a gun?" recalling our conversations over the last year and a half. MMJ just smiled and said, "He is just a man from Uruzgan." I chuckled and gave him a hug and told him we would talk later.

Everyone began to take their seats, with Col. Gilliam and I sitting at the opposite end of the room from the Hamkar, and the judges just as MK entered the room. Though all rose, MK went straight to MMJ to greet him first, hand kiss and all. The signal had been given. I sat back in my chair, poised to take notes from Ulmary, my interpreter.

As MMJ opened the proceedings with an opening prayer, I felt like I was drifting into a new world. *They have set sail on their own course*, I thought. The PGOV, a man not from Uruzgan, was left by "his" legal shura on the dock that day.

Haji Abdul Wahid read the agenda, and it included everything—Hamkar's indiscretion, checkpoint commanders' poor treatment of the population, better prosecutor and police cooperation, and the establishment of a women's shelter. That last item almost knocked me over, given the harsh resistance to such shelters throughout rural Afghanistan, but it explained the presence of the DOWA. I would learn later that Dr. Stanikzai had gone from Hamkar to Haji Abdul Wahid, to MMJ and MK, discussing the issues that they could agree on that should be covered. He had taken it upon his shoulders to build a functioning justice system in Uruzgan, at least in the capital of Tarin Kowt.

Left to right: Hamkar, MMJ, Haji Abdul Wahid, Col Hanif, unknown, Mohammad Zai, unknown, MK

This would not go unnoticed by the Taliban, and he would live under the constant threat of death. However, he was under the protection of MMJ and MK and realized that the more the legal sector functioned as one, not only would the human rights conditions improve but so would his safety. The entire shura was very open and produced much discussion. It was as if all the issues that were frustrated by the lack of the provincial chief of police's presence in the past had come rushing forward.

The most agitated and eventually most productive revolved around the issues between Hamkar and Haji Abdul Wahid. You could see the stress in Hamkar's body language, with his right hand constantly going to his head. However, Hamkar showed his character and education by not backing down an inch concerning the issues that caused him to go to Kabul. However, his savvy showed by agreeing to keep things local. Everyone agreed that they would "place a stone" so the matter could be resolved.

Dr. Stanikzai, MK, Abdul Raziq (son-in-law to HAW),
Hamkar, and MMJ

Placing a stone was done to symbolize that no tribes could take any actions during the time the stone was in place—a cooling-off period for negotiations to take place. Haji Abdul Wahid Achekzai, the most corrupt of the judges, stated, "Solve Hamkar's problem, you solve mine." Another civil prosecutor would replace Hamkar in March 2013. That one was gone by June 2014. As of November 2014, Achekzai was still there.

Left to right: Col. Habibi, MOJ Abdul Baqi, the author, Col. Gilliam, interpreter, prison Director Jammuddin, unknown

It was particularly satisfying to be there with Col. Gilliam. He was passionate about his mission, and he loved his soldiers. I can only imagine the depths of his sorrow over the deaths of his troops at the hands of a suicide bomber outside the Tarin Kowt police substation shortly after they had arrived. Though he wasn't part of the earlier efforts to bring the justice sector together to form a functioning criminal justice sector, we were a team. He and his unit of police mentors made strong contributions that helped the CoPP efforts. The cooperation between prosecutors and police was a major factor in building trust within the criminal justice system, and that trust was essential to the legal shura's success. This was a victory that came at a high cost.

Kabul Rule of Law Conference 2012: Wrap It Up

Two days after the Uruzgan legal shura, I was in Kabul on the ISAF side of Kabul International Airport. This was to be the last gathering of the field rule of law advisors, for RoL Ambassador Steve McFarland's message was clear. Focus on what was necessary, achievable, and sustainable. He indicated that all field locations would be closed by June 2014. I knew UPRT was closing down by December 2013, and I had asked to remain until it closed to finish out all we had started. However, with the strong start of the "new" legal shura back in Uruzgan, I was very optimistic that what was going to be accomplished that fit that criteria had been. Everything from this point forward was all gravy. The annoying fly buzzing around me concerning the achievable and sustainable directive was the new commanding general of Regional Command South, General Abrams.

Gen. Abrams had come aboard a few months earlier with a rule of law burr under his saddle. Directions came fast and furious for all PRTs, including UPRT, to institute trial monitoring, prosecutor and police joint training, and tracking of prisoners and cases. The frustration came with his legal team's response to our assertions that all of those initiatives had been accomplished, in some cases over a year earlier. It was one of absolute disbelief and demands that we prove all that we said. There was a matrix that had to be completed with dates and activities that could be used in a Power Point presentation. Catch-22 was alive and well. I was fit to be tied. As frustrating as it was, we were blessed with a core group of fine Australian junior officers who sat down with me and took all UPRT's information and backfilled the matrix. We were done in just a few weeks, and most of that time was spent gathering the information from the military prison side of the base run by the Australians.

The more disturbing news was the reports of corruption, and its depth, that US Ambassador Cunningham set before us. The GNP of Afghanistan was $15 billion, and $4 billion of that was being siphoned off. Corruption was undermining everything. The attorney general's office was "corrupt with a capital C." So with the ministry that was in charge of all civil investigation in the Afghan legal system so corrupt, what did the future hold? It wasn't hard to see why the Uruzganis didn't trust the AGO prosecutor in Tarin Kowt when his minister was so tainted. Mental exhaustion started to set in, for the next two days of the conference was a blur. Given the time we had left, one thing was very clear to me. Stability in Uruzgan would mean a stop-gap hybrid system where a broad enough spectrum of tribal elders was vested in MK's survival, and MK would have to see that his survival was dependent on a greater functioning criminal justice system that protected civil society and human rights. The religious leaders were the key, and my Afghan hero that would fill that role was the Toki tribal leader and chief judge, Malavi Mohammad Jan.

The Most Powerful Man in Uruzgan

Returning from Kabul, I received an urgent call two days later from Dr. Stanikzai. His regional director, a Dr. Bidar, had come to Uruzgan to meet the legal shura members. The Uruzgan AIHRC had received recognition for its achievement in the area of human rights, and he wanted to personally thank all involved. Dr. Stanikzai wanted him to meet me before the legal shura, which had been set by the Afghans for October 6, just three weeks after the last one. We set a meeting for the next day, October 3.

Dr. Bidar and Dr. Stanikzai were cut from the same cloth—shaven, cosmopolitan for an Afghan, and very well spoken. When we met, Dr. Bidar asked me, "Why do you men from the US State Department all have beards?" I explained to him that in Uruzgan a man has a beard and an old man had a gray one. Since I was an outsider, it helped to present myself in the most culturally acceptable manner. If I was in Kabul, maybe I wouldn't have one, but I wasn't. He just laughed, nodding his head while acknowledging all that I said as true.

Drs. Bidar and Stanikzai had been very busy since he had arrived. They had met together with both MMJ and Abdul Hadi Hamkar. Dr. Stanikzai knew that bringing the civil prosecutor into good relations with the judges and police was essential. Hamkar was frustrated and wanted to resign. A local member of parliament, Abdullah Barackzai, was pushing to get Hamkar out and returning Mustafa. Dr. Bidar had talked him into waiting things out. So much progress was being made, and the real work was just starting. They had also meet for several hours with MK where the main focus was the Afghan Local Police (ALP). These were the groups the US-SOF worked with. The Khas Uruzgan ALP groups headed by the Hazaran, Shujai and the Pashtu,

Ruy Mohammad were still a source of concern for AIHRC as well as MK.

I asked Dr. Stanikzai his opinion of how the justice sector was coming together. He reported that low-level ANP were being held accountable for misbehavior and that judges were hearing cases concerning violence against women. Those were two big steps forward. I asked him about his perception of the success of MMJ's efforts with bringing the tribal and formal justice together. He paused and said so much had changed concerning MMJ since 2010, when I first arrived. Then, he feared to set foot outside his court or housing complex. However, today, "MMJ is the most powerful man in Uruzgan. No person can resist him, not even the governor." It was a tribal power based on his true humility and recognized religious authority. Dr. Stanikzai told me MMJ can walk anywhere in Tarin Kowt without fear. All the people see what he has accomplished for all the people of Uruzgan. The people call him with any threats to his safety. Remembering he didn't want to have the responsibility for "even the dogs in the street" that a provincial governor must have, he surely found a way around taking care of the dogs.

A Citizen of Afghanistan

Three days later, we gathered again within the provincial police compound headquarters building. With such an honored guest, the room was packed. MMJ was already in his seat by the time I had arrived. I knew there was to be a meeting between MMJ, MK, Hamkar, and Dr. Bidar before the shura began. Going over to MMJ, he looked tired. He often had moments of a near exhausted aura around him. This was one of those times. I leaned over him, signaling him not to rise, and we embraced. We spoke briefly about his health and that of his family. He asked the same of me. MK then entered the room and came over to greet MMJ formally, and then the meeting got started.

This shura was highlighted by the theme of togetherness and praise for MK. Speeches concerning Islam's dictates that they act united, that Mohammad sought advice and counsel from all around him, that MK faced many issues, that those who seek advice will be successful, and that no one lives forever. This was much like the advice from the slave holding the laurel crown above the Roman conquering general that all glory is fleeting. I was optimistically hoping that Hamkar would remain in Uruzgan when he spoke of the shura being the place where all could work together for the common good, helping each other accomplish a good justice system. The issue of a women's shelter was raised again, and MK ordered that a home be found near the police headquarters compound. He stated he would fund and protect it, but the DOWA would operate it. The Bibi Aisha case was raised by Hamkar, and the group agreed that sending ANP into the region would cost lives, and it was best to hold on that for now. It was curious to hear MK vocalize the allegations that the former prosecutor, Mustafa, was corrupt and taking bribes. This was a definite nod toward the acceptance of Hamkar. MMJ gave voice to the known fact that there were many problems that would take a long time to work through, and all agreed that they needed to meet every two to four weeks to keep the process moving forward. Abdul Baqi from the MOJ spoke of the need for blankets for the juvenile prisoners this winter. MK, with a wave of his hand, said, "I will send them to you." There was much praise for MK and his generosity, which told me the group was putting on a show for the important guest. As things were winding down, MMJ asked me for my input.

This took me a bit by surprise, but it was in the tradition of the early days of the shura at the appeals court. I paused for a moment to gather my thoughts. When I spoke, I became acutely aware that I had become invested in this group of people here in Uruzgan. I knew instinctively what was expected from me with Dr. Bidar attending. There was some hope of getting an NGO, and thus international funding, to establish a women's shelter. I had spoken of this with Dr. Stanikzai, so I told the group that I would continue to work on that. I joined in the praise of MK by pointing out to the group that MK was the first PCOP to join in the efforts of the legal shura. I reminded them of the days when we would end such meetings, knowing that without the PCOP's support many of the things they were trying to accomplish could not be done. Looking directly at MMJ, I said we must acknowledge MK for his participation. Then I looked at MK and praised MMJ for having the wisdom and patience that allowed this legal shura to become such a positive influence in Uruzgan. It would take the group's combined wisdom and patience to maintain this shura for all the generations that will follow them. Everyone nodded in agreement. We adjourned for lunch with an agreement they would meet again in two weeks.

I spent lunch next to Abdul Mohammad and his bird song telephone, which would go silent in March 2015, as he and his son would be assassinated in a targeted ambush after the main Australian forces left the region. I became aware of how normal it felt sitting next to someone where we could only communicate through sign language and a smile, eating with my hands, with flatbread serving as my utensils. I had gone native to a greater extent than I had even realized. As Dr. Stanikzai would say to me, I had done things the Afghan way and in the process had become a citizen of Afghanistan.

The Pain and the Joy of It All

I didn't see MMJ for another week, but when I did, it was obvious that he had regained his strength. I brought a member of the base-run Radio Uruzgan for him to record an Eid message. It would be his third radio message in six months. He obviously no longer kept a low profile, as was the case back in 2010. After his message was recorded, he talked to me about how Taliban commanders in Quetta, Pakistan, who wished to reintegrate with the Afghan government, were being killed or arrested. He stated that the former prime minister of Pakistan, Benazir Bhutto, was killed for her position, in her campaign to again be reelected to that position, of noninterference with the internal politics of Afghanistan. To the end of my time there, he would insist that our real enemy was the Pakistan ISI.

He had pulled back the "idiot judge" Abdul Wahid from Deh Rawud for his own safety. More importantly, he and MK engaged directly with each other every week. He then stated something that will always stick with me. In speaking with him about the Taliban leaders, he stated that they would be extended a peace offering three times over, as required by Islamic sharia. After that, they would be killed. I often thought about how power politics have always been conducted here, that constant conflict and negotiations with the threat of violence always in the background. He must have felt very confident that the Taliban were not strong enough to take back Uruzgan, which meant he felt MK was powerful enough to deliver security even though we were leaving.

The next weeks went by with uneventful meetings. Then a crushing emotional blow descended upon Camp Ripley in late October. Three members of the command were killed on the same day in two different incidents. A Navy SEAL was killed in an operation, and two civil affairs soldiers were shot in Khas Uruzgan: Kantor, a Jew; Kashif, "Kash", a Muslim; and Ruiz, a Christian. They came to symbolize for us all what we as a diverse society treasure. It nearly broke my spirit. As much as you don't let on it affects you, it does, deeply. We would go about our business that day in a quiet, efficient stupor. "Fast Eddie" kept me posted as to when they would be putting Kashif on the C-130. I don't remember the time, but it was late, and the night was cold. We walked out from Camp Ripley to the tarmac. We stood out on the tarmac in a mixed formation of civilian and military, old and young, as the C-130 taxied in and dropped its rear-loading hatch, awaiting its precious cargo. The group grew as the ambulance carrying Kash approached. The crimson-bereted SAS soldiers from TF-66 started to appear out of the darkness as if summoned by our heavy hearts. We formed two lines of a long, informal honor guard through which the stretcher baring the body-bagged, honored dead passed. Once the body was secured, we filed in six at a time, three to a side, to render our final honors and farewells. We waited for the doors of the aircraft to secure and then taxi out to the runway. I remembered the half-dirt, half-concrete lifeline that greeted me two years ago, now transformed into a solid band of concrete, bearing heavy cargo planes loaded with all the needed supplies for such a remote base. It now held the vibrating aircraft solidly as it raced down its length with the most precious cargo of all, a fallen soldier. As it lifted into the dark heavens, I felt my heart crushing. Nothing was said going back to Camp Ripley.

Over the next weeks, meetings concerning the juvenile detention center and the court filled my calendar, keeping me busy. I had been invited to the appeals court for an Eid celebration lunch with MMJ and many from the legal shura. Our PRT director, Adrian, had asked to attend to get to know MMJ on a more social level. That request thrilled me because I was constantly beating the drum of his soft power influencing much of what was happening in the province. At the last minute, Adrian was called out on a security issue concerning one of our MRAPs carrying AusAID personnel hitting an IED. Thank God no one was injured even though the tires were blown five hundred meters to either side of the vehicle.

The meal was very light, reflecting a traditional Toki farm Eid meal of yogurt, mint, and berries. Dr. Stanikzai was there, and I spent a very pleasant time sitting next to MMJ and just generally conversing on family issues. We kept it light, with my only inquiry being how MK was progressing in becoming an elder of Uruzgan. MMJ informed me that it was likely he would succeed with a little help. As I took my leave that day, I handed to MMJ one hundred US dollars. He looked at me with a puzzled look. I told him it was an Eid offering for the poor people of Uruzgan and that he would know how to deliver it to those who needed it. He smiled and said in Pashtu, "Yes, yes, yes," a sound that came out sounding like "Yoish, youish, youish." We had exchanged a few gifts over the last two years. I brought him a handmade Native American Woodlands pipe with a horned bowl early in 2011. Subsequently, I received a very warm wool wrap that was traditionally used in the region where heat was a luxury. He wore one consistently from November through to the warming of spring weather.

On November 6, 2012, a service for Kantor, Kashif, and Ruiz was held. It was a Friday warmed by the sun. The usual list of dignitaries came from Kandahar. It was sadly unique with its mix of Jewish, Muslim, and Christian prayers. I was on a flight to Kabul the next morning, heading home for R&R.

I was emotionally exhausted and glad to be heading home for a rest. I had been assured that my extension should go through since the senior civilian representative in RC-S, Ambassador Addleton, had given his approval. I was preparing myself for the final push to strengthen the legal shura before we pulled out.

Sequester, the Great Experiment Ends

"You were the one person the UPRT director wanted to extend. Amb. Addleton had placed you on his list of persons to be approved, but the embassy came back and said make the cuts deeper." The words from Rob, the senior US State Department person on the UPRT, spoken to me on Pearl Harbor Day 2012 stopped me in my tracks as I reentered the "bomb shelter" office space we shared. Rob had come on in July, and even then, he was told he would be the last. UPRT was scheduled to stand down no later than November 2013. Congress was heading for a deadlock that seemed certain to trigger the poison pill of the "sequestration." These were across-the-board cuts in all US government agencies, and State was slimming down in advance of the March 1 implementation date. All contracts of non-career US State Department personnel not considered essential were not going to be renewed. Mine ended January 19, 2013. I was to be prepared to be in Kabul on January 10 to allow time to process out. From a mission standpoint, it made no sense, but I had seen this exhausted knee-jerk show before, back in the early 1970s as we pulled out of Vietnam. Support for this engagement had collapsed in the States, and that was that. I would have enough time to say my good-byes and pass off to the Australians as much as I could. However, it signaled the end of engagement with the legal shura. Keeping Niebuhr's prayer in mind, I set out a thirty-day agenda and prepared to leave.

A few days later, as I passed by the SOF commander's office, CMDR Price, I stuck my head in to give him the news. I said something along the lines that the mission had shifted due to financial constraints. This was going to wind down fast and to just keep himself and his people as safe as he could. We shook hands, and I sensed a sadness in the room. I almost turned to ask if he was okay, but I shrugged it off and walked out the door. Days later, CMDR Price would take his own life. A pallor of grief would hang over Christmas as we all searched our souls to answer the question, why? Maybe it was the huge loss of three under his command on the same day, but really it had become an epidemic among US forces' veterans. Years of multiple deployments into these combat zones has a devastating toll on those who serve.

Ten Thousand Rifles Cannot Protect You

After meeting with Dr. Stanikzai, I learned that a few days before I arrived back in Uruzgan, a vehicle-borne IED had killed thirteen people near the National Directorate of Security crossing just down from the appeals court. The target was MMJ, but he had been tipped off about the attempt on his life and had taken another route to the court that day. There was better news in that three judges had been dispatched to Deh Rawud, the "idiot" among them. However, he now had well-educated judges to keep him in check. There had been a confrontation between the civil prosecutor's office and the ANP. It seemed Hamkar had nullified a six-year-old being married off. Such marriages were contrary to Afghan law but still not unknown in the remote rural areas. The husband's brother was an ANP officer, and he surrounded the prosecutor's compound, threatening to shoot Hamkar. MK had stepped in and stopped the action. The issue would be brought up at the next legal shura. As bad as this may sound, it was a breakthrough because MK didn't move to a solution but deferred it to the group setting. The next legal shura was set for December 10, just two days away. "It will be my last one, Dr. Stanikzai" were my words that brought a stunned silence from him. Maybe it drove home the obvious truth of the pullout he had been dreading, for his safety would be at further risk. He recovered quickly and said he would arrange a farewell luncheon.

Arriving at the PHQ building where the legal shura now called home, I could tell I was becoming retrospective. My time was ending here, and I was struggling to leave this meeting with just one thing that the whole group could hold onto and use to their advantage. Hamkar would not attend this shura; I had met with Hamkar just the day before to say my good-byes. When I walked into his compound, he greeted me warmly but with unusual reserve. I could see that his head and beard had been shaved, and the hair was just now growing back. This was an Afghan grief ritual. His wife of forty years had recently died. He had spoken of her to me in the past with pride. She was his only wife and had borne several children that she raised to be successful young adults. His grief was obvious, and we spent the time speaking of her and her accomplishments. I genuinely liked this man and had grown fond of him and his poetry.

When MMJ came into the room, he strolled directly toward me. We embraced, and then he told me that he had heard that I was leaving. I held the sadness in me at bay as I told him that I had expected to stay until nearly this time next year, but the drawdown for me was coming sooner than expected. He told me that he looked forward to Dr. Stanikzai's farewell luncheon.

The meeting got off to a good start. The women's shelter issue was still on the agenda and was making progress. The issue of the six-year-old girl was brought before the group. A new revelation exposed a scheme where the father had promised her to several families and collected "baad," bride price, from each. Dr. Stanikzai moved for the ANP to take the girl, and MMJ interjected "with a proper warrant," to the DOWA until the matter could be resolved. MMJ spoke of the law under the constitution; clearly such a compulsive marriage was not allowed. It was good to see the positive discussion was going to lead to action.

Police misconduct then was raised, specifically one of MK's checkpoint commanders who had many complaints against him. MK owed this man loyalty and was part of his patronage network. He was struggling with taking action against him. MK was seated in front of MMJ, talking to him about the issue. I could see the struggle in his eyes. I pulled my chair up and motioned to Ulmaryee, my interpreter, to come up next to me. I placed my hand on MK's left thigh as I leaned forward. This was a presumptuous act. He turned to me, and those dark eyes penetrated through me. I said, "Matiullah, this is a problem that police chiefs around the world face. Good commanders in the field are hard to come by, but he wears the uniform that represents you. What he does either honors or dishonors you. What is important is not that you punish him but that you call him to account for his actions. Bring him in publicly so the people can see you stand with them. Let MMJ and the other members of the legal shura help you with this. Don't take it all on yourself. Spread the burden. Let this shura speak as one, as the community. Ten thousand rifles can't protect you and the members of this shura better than a million eyes and ears connected to hearts that want you to live."

Looking at MMJ, I could see his reaction as Ulmaryee finished translating. He nodded his head in agreement, saying in Pashtu, "Yes, yes, yes."

I smiled at Matiullah, and he at me, as I said, "You are more today than you were a year ago. You are a mix of the old and new ways. Keep the graybeards close and listen to their wisdom as you move forward as provincial chief of police."

MK said he would bring in all his district chiefs of police and checkpoint commanders for talks. As I pulled my chair back, MK spoke of his desire for literacy training for all police as a way to curb abuse. He himself was undergoing private tutoring. You could see the label of illiterate used to demean him was going to fall by the wayside.

The shura finished strong with a wide range of issues being discussed, including corruption and getting judges out to districts with long-overdue police protection.

I would have one more mission out to the provincial court to introduce Rob to MMJ. The leadership of UPRT was scrambling to not lose this line of engagement, but that horse had left the barn. There wasn't really even the need for me, as the next year and a half would show. The legal shura was rolling along. I had met the goal of working myself out of a job.

"They Consider You Their Friend"

Setting a mission to go out to Tarin Kowt to have a farewell lunch bore some thought. The location of the lunch was the AIHRC building, which lay directly across from the civil prosecutor's office. This was only fifty yards from the location of the suicide bombing that took place at the Tarin Kowt ANP substation that took the lives of Col. Gilliam's men. This was an open street that was well traveled. That meant a car could make a run at the compound with a high probability of success. I took some extra time with our OGA security platoon to go over the particulars and to make sure they felt comfortable with the mission. They set out a plan that would use the Bushies to limit access to the street from both ends. We would be there for about three hours, so I wanted them to be sure they were comfortable with the risk. Adrian, the senior civilian from UPRT, would be coming with me to meet with MMJ.

The day came, and we stepped off at 1100 hours. This would be my final ride in a Bushie, and I was thinking about my first one back in December 2010 and all that had transpired since then with this group where I was going to say farewell. Looking out the front window at the usual Tarin Kowt traffic, I wondered as always how these people would fare over the next years. I watched the looks in the eyes of those we passed by and thought about how out of place these large vehicles must look to them. Arriving at the AIHRC office, we waited until the convoy commander gave us the go-ahead to dismount. Getting out of the Bushie, I could see how the lead and rear Bushies had barricaded the road, leaving us a relatively secure area with the AIHRC gate in the middle. Adrian and I first went in the AIHRC compound and were met by Dr. Stanikzai. He was very excited to have us and directed us into a room he had set up for the lunch.

Hamkar and several of his assistants were the first to arrive. His hair and beard were well on the way to growing back. Mohammand Zai, the military internal affairs prosecutor, came next. We embraced, and right behind him came MMJ and Mirwais Ghani, the chief civil prosecutor when I first arrived but who now was the appeals prosecutor. Regretfully absent were Haji Abdul Wahid and his son-in-law Abdul Razeeq. They were still the focus of MMJ's attempts at cleaning up the judiciary, and the friction was strong. Several of Col Hanif's assistants who had taken the CoPP course arrived with Col Hanif's regrets for not attending. With Hamkar on one side and MMJ on the other, I sat down to enjoy our last time together.

Hamkar on the author's right; to his left, MMJ, Adrian, and Ulmaryee

MMJ opened the meal with a prayer, and Dr. Stanikzai brought in the food. There was much small talk around the table between Mohammad Zai and myself as I queried him on personal matters he and I had discussed back 2011. I caught up with MMJ on how his family was doing, and I inquired on his ability to see his daughters and their families over the Eid holiday. It was difficult for him to get to see them in the past. However, he had seen them just recently because the area was safer to travel to now. I could see a very confident MMJ sitting next to me. The PRT director, Adrian, was asking MMJ several questions, and I found myself filling in areas of his response to give Adrian a better context for what MMJ was saying. I found myself reminiscing with Mirwais about the Bibi Aisha case, the old prosecutor's office with the roof that was always threatening to collapse upon us, and the car buried in front of that building. Two-plus years of my life spent with them could be seen in the body language and the jovial bantering among us going around the table. Mohamad Zai specifically was very praising for the all the training that had been brought in during my time. We spoke of Jan Wilken and the Dutch EUPOL team as well as the upcoming transition. I praised MMJ and all there for their efforts in getting the legal shura operating on a regular basis.

The time went by quickly, and when it came time for good-byes, I could feel my heart being tugged by what I was about to be leaving. I watched MMJ as we adjourned to the courtyard area just inside the gate to the AIHRC compound. He seemed proud and in control as we took many final pictures. He would come to Camp Holland two days later to deliver to me a gift so personal he couldn't give it to me at this event. I had recently remarried while home on leave, and he presented me with a bright crimson Afghan outfit for my wife. He said at the time he gave it to me, "It is for your wife, but it is for you." Haris, our State Department cultural advisor, told me afterward it is the type of gift that only very close friends give to each other and MMJ must think of me as a brother because such a gift was extremely personal. On this day as I took my final pictures with MMJ and watched him walk out the compound gate, erect and proud, confidently going to his nearby armored SUV, I felt all that and more. Adrian took me aside before we left and said, "You can see that they consider you their friend. I doubted your approach when I first encountered what you and Richelle had set out in the roadmap, but I can see it worked."

MMJ and assistant prosecutors

I told him of my deeply held belief that "people don't care what you know until they know that you care." My greatest frustration was the lack of caring we, as a coalition of nations, really had for these people in the context of their own culture. Too much time was wasted on efforts to make them like us, a total impossibility, rather than work within the cultural context to develop their systems to a point where they could meet international norms with systems of government that they develop themselves.

"Any Place You Need Your Blood Type on Your Jacket"

Other than MMJ's final visit, with his gift for my wife (which was to say for me), the final days on MNBTK went by in a blur. Getting items mailed back to the States, my information turned over to Rob and others, my CHU to Bob from USAID, and a final good-bye to all on Ripley, culminating with suddenly being on the tarmac awaiting the final Embassy Air flight to Kabul. That morning, I had given away all my gloves, except one pair, to the Afghan guards on Ripley who were always huddled around a small fire during the cold nights. I had made it a habit of bringing them cigarettes every evening when I came over from Camp Holland, at first motivated by just being a nice person and showing my appreciation for their work, but as the blue-on-green incidents increased, it became more of a self-survival insurance premium. Getting on the aircraft for the last time, I thought of the air-charter services personnel that operated the service we called Embassy Air who were killed as suicide bomber rammed their van in Kabul as it was on its way to take the crew and ground personnel into KIA one morning. As the aircraft taxied down the runway of MNBTK, I just felt the weight of all the stored grief in me start to flow out in silent tears coursing down my cheeks, to be absorbed by my ever-present Afghan scarf around my neck. One more use for that ever-present utilitarian garment.

The week at the embassy in Kabul was uneventful. All who were at the embassy when I had first arrived in November 2010 had long since departed. After a week of unloading my personal protective gear, transponder GPS tracker, and cell phone, I felt stripped bare. I got in the SUV for my final drive through Kabul traffic to KIA. Watching the congestion engulf us, I couldn't help but have visions of a suicide bomber getting close enough to detonate. I was experiencing the short-timer's jitters. This was not an irrational fear, given upon my arrival back in 2010, I was informed of the frequency of attacks between the embassy and the airport. Making my way into the terminal at KIA, I made it through the multiple security checkpoints as quickly as possible just to sit in the crowded waiting area, filled to the brim with passengers awaiting the several flights going to Dubai. I found some agreeable companions to pass the time with, and we were soon off to Dubai.

Boarding the plane in Dubai for DC, I was just too tired to do anything but sleep, a rare reprieve in that long flight. I did think about how quickly my time in Washington, DC, would go, just as it had when coming home from Iraq. After customs, I would transfer my bags from the Dubai flight to the one going to Detroit. Then grabbing a cab into DC, at about 0800 hours, I would go to Navy Hill to process out. This time I would actually pick up some certificates of service signed by US Secretary of State Hillary Rodham Clinton, which was a nice gesture. I would be back in a cab heading for Dulles International by noon. I would be home with my feet up by ten o'clock at night. Living in this age of being able to be anywhere in the world in two days still amazes and scares me at the same time.

As my plane from Dubai landed in Washington, DC, with all that yet in front of me, I put on my old weather-beaten leather USMC flight jacket, grabbed my carry-on backpack, and made my way down to immigration. Standing in the long line waiting my turn with the Homeland Security officer, I was going through my checklist of all that I had to do before coming back to Dulles. When it came my turn to pass through the passport control, I walked up and gave the officer my passport. He scanned my passport and looked up at me and stated, "Any place where you have to wear your blood type on your jacket must be a dangerous place." Somewhat confused, I followed his eyes that were looking at the cloth nametag sewed on the left breast of my jacket. It had been a gift from the person at the embassy who first cared for the Uruzgan personnel back in 2010. There, next to the embroidered Department of State logo, was "Crowther," "PRT-Uruzgan," a red cross symbol, and then, "A POS-1945." All the information a combat medic needed should I become wounded. I just looked at the officer and smiled, saying, "Yes, some days it was."

Epilogue

In June 2014, while I was working with "moderate Syrians" in Gaziantep, Turkey, the news erupted with a new group "with the wrong sharia" grabbing the headlines. The "Islamic State" invaded the western regions of Iraq with explosive results. The slow, simmering anger against the Shia regime of Iraqi President Maliki had exploded, and a mere eight hundred IS fighters joined by Iraqi Sunnis had the Iraqi Army on the run. In the weeks that followed, American and British citizens were beheaded on camera, and Christian and non-Muslim sects were told to leave areas of Iraq taken by this new group, convert to Salafist Islam or die. However, not all options were always given. Shias and Christians fled or died. The ring of "Allah Akbar," "God is great" is louder than ever, with tribes in Helmand and Zabul, Afghanistan lifting the flag of the Islamic State and attacking Taliban as well as Afghan government forces. Paris, France, came under attack by Al-Qaida terrorists, and Verviers, Belgium, has seen a preemptive strike against Islamic-State-trained jihadist. The world still fails to understand what drives these brutal religious zealots. Worse is the fact they, and not the moderates, are winning a media war that is shaping the dynamics toward a major, bloody conflict. I fear the worst and pray for better times.

Papers are being written asking the question of whether the Taliban will embrace a compromise with the Kabul government and recognize any constitutional government in Afghanistan. I can only point out that historically a deal between and among all the tribes of Afghanistan will determine that. In the end, the diverse regions will remain autonomous, and whatever government holds power in Kabul, it will be based on a confederacy of self-interests and the art of the deal.

However, in a remote region of Afghanistan, in a town few outsiders have ever heard of, more changes have occurred, some with great promise, others showing the ever-present brute force underlying everything.

The Combined Team Uruzgan headed by the Australian conventional forces lowered their flags over Camp Holland in late 2013. The withdrawal coincided with the harsh winter, which would keep the Talib in Pakistan until the snows of the mountain passes melted in the spring of 2015. During that time, massive protests by civil society groups occurred, made up of mostly young people, forcing the provincial governor, Amir Achundzada, to step down. A local person replaced him by the name of Amanullah Timore. Amanullah is from Gizab, which is in northern Uruzgan, and hails from the Hazaran tribe. This was a real change in the Pashtu power politics but one that I am sure MMJ had a hand in. He and other tribal elders had been called to Kabul to discuss the situation that gave rise to the protests, and this choice is consistent with his expansive, inclusive position with all the tribes. Timore's Hazaran credentials did bring Sujay's Khas Uruzgan militia closer to working with those in Tarin Kowt. It seems a good deal among the Uruzgan tribes. The legal shura continued to strengthen strong, and the formal justice sector pushed out from Tarin Kowt into Khas Uruzgan suggested that that was part of the deal. Qazi Abdul Razeeq, formally the number-two judge in the Tarin Kowt primary court and former mujahedeen, was placed in Chora. In the past, when MMJ sent one of the new young judges out there, the first night letter would send them running back to TK. Abdul Razeeq's "muj" credentials sends a strong message. Also, he is Acheckzai's son-in-law, and the Achekzai tribe is strong in Chora. Three judges are in Deh Rawud. The expansion of better-trained and educated traditional tribal shuras that are working with MMJ seemed to be forcing the Talib courts out of Uruzgan. A large caseload was reported by mid-2014 with six hundred to seven hundred cases, and with 2013 (Afghan year 1391) being cut short, the 1100 cases reported was impressive. When I left, there were twelve functioning judges, thirteen if you count old Mohammad Doad up in Chora. According to a recent letter from MMJ, he now has nineteen. That was a big jump.

The Ministry of Justice appointed a local person from Tarin Kowt as a public defender. He was a graduate of the Sharia Law Faculty at

Kandahar University. His name is Esamtullah Osmai, from the Toori Village of the Tarin Kowt area.

MMJ is openly working with the traditional tribal elders to have their rulings at shuras conform to proper Hanifi sharia and the laws of Afghanistan. He continues to create a criminal referral system from these shuras.

Women's issues continued to be mostly handled by the tribal elders, but there have been huge strides made in protecting women from abuse, as evidenced by the continued efforts to create a women's shelter by the legal shura/justice sector, which includes the AIHRC. Sadly, Dr. Stanikzai's success made him a target for Taliban attacks. After an unsuccessful assassination attempt in his home province in September 2014, he resigned from his position and now lives in Australia under a program to bring those who worked with Australians, and are under threat, to the safety of Australia. I hope the actions of Islamist terrorists there and in Europe don't blow back on this kind, hardworking man or his family. That would be a sad, tragic irony.

Haris remained in Kandahar working hard for the success of his country until June 2015. He and his immediate family now live in America under our State Department program.

The AGO / civil prosecutor's office always struggled with getting on board with how things are done in Uruzgan. The single most frustrating behavior coming from each chief AGO prosecutor since Mustafar, an outsider, took over from Salihi, an insider and a member of MK's tribe, was their arrogant behavior toward the rural people of the region. Mustafar, Hamkar, and Hamkar's replacement, Rawoothi, all had this issue. Rawoothi left Uruzgan in June 2014. However, January 2015 saw MMJ's influence bear fruit once again. The legal shura brought the new PGOV into the fold, and the AGO / civil prosecutor's office received five new professional prosecutors. They targeted corruption within several ministry directors' offices, the Deh Rawud district governor, and some police officers. All this was supported by MMJ and the PGOV. This action drew strong support from tribal leaders and the youth of Uruzgan.

The MMJ and the legal shura, working as a unit, brought together all of Uruzgan, including tribal leaders formerly aligned with the Taliban and the Hazaran Khas Uruzgan militia commander, Sujay. The criminal acts of the Taliban in the area are drawing anger and criticism from their former supporters. They formed their own local forces aligned with ANP and ANA to bring stability to their villages.

However, a seismic shift occurred in March 2015. PCOP Matiullah Khan, the Emperor of Uruzgan, was killed while visiting Kabul. Some say by the hands of a suicide bomber, but my source says a government ministry vehicle took him to a meeting with a high-ranking government official. His body was found several days later in a Kabul side street. This leaves a huge power vacuum in Uruzgan. The ministry of interior tried to return Juma Gul to his old post as the PCOP, but MMJ and the elders stepped in to stop that. Colonel Gulab, the professional, scotch-drinking police investigator, was appointed as a temporary PCOP. A few weeks later, he was killed, reported by the news as an IED, but my sources said it was a Taliban attack.

Omar Khan fled to Kabul after MK was killed. A new professional PCOP by the name of Tooryali Abdiani has been appointed as well as a new PGOV Mohammad Nazir Kharoli. Both are heavily engaged with the legal shura and the group has a regular television show where local issues are discussed and people call in with their concerns. This is a strong direct connection with their Uruzgan government that weakens any hold outsiders would wish to exert. The youth are heavily engaged in this project.

In the background is the brother of MK, Haji Rahimullah. He holds the loyalty of all of MK's commanders and most of his former KAU police. He currently holds the position of Police HQ security commander and his power is growing every day. Like MK I believe he will soon be named the new PCOP.

Mullah Omar is now dead and the Taliban face being replaced by ISIS groups. The proper sharia conflict morphs once again. The ANA, ANP and Taliban are engaging in fierce battles in Uruzgan, and the legal shura is still a target. This sacred piece of remote dirt, the place where Mullah Omar was raised, is locked in that struggle. MMJ has met with the new president, Ashraf Ghani Ahmadzai, and established strong ties as he continues to be the voice of "proper sharia." Most of the NGOs have left and jobs are scarce. Will the opium money replace the NGO cash flow for the people?

Tarburwali still is the rule of the land, and God's authority trumps all. MMJ, the Malavi, saw it coming and brought together all the tribal cousins to weather the storm. They stand against all outsiders, including the Talib, who would take advantage of the people of Uruzgan. Col. Hanif is standing stern and strong at MMJ's side. Hopefully Matiullah Khan's brother will "make the deal" and be approved by the Malavi and the elders. The battle is far from over. The big question is who controls the opium now? I pray the legal shura members control it, for they will need the power of the economy that it provides to survive. The irony is I now sit in court here in Toledo, Ohio, as the criminal docket in any given day reflects the large increase in heroin usage in the United States. The dust devils of Uruzgan are feeding a tornado of heroin drug addiction here in my hometown. Solutions are difficult, with competing needs involving the lives of populations. Our country's competing interests clash. I close my eyes, and I can see the tall columns of dust rising across the arid land, dancing their ageless dance.

Printed in the United States
By Bookmasters